W9-APS-586

CRYSTALS

CRYSTALS

THE SCIENCE, MYSTERIES, AND LORE

DOUGLAS BULLIS

CRESCENT BOOKS
New York

A FRIEDMAN GROUP BOOK

This 1990 edition published by Crescent Books
distributed by Outlet Book Company, Inc., a Random House Company
225 Park Avenue South
New York, New York 10003

Copyright © 1990 by Michael Friedman Publishing Group, Inc.

All rights reserved. No part of this publication may be
reproduced, stored in a retrieval system or transmitted, in any
form or by any means, electronic, mechanical, photocopying,
recording or otherwise, without the prior written permission of
the publisher.

CRYSTALS: The Science, Mysteries, and Lore
was prepared and produced by
Michael Friedman Publishing Group, Inc.
15 West 26th Street
New York, New York 10010

Editor: Melissa Schwarz
Art Director: Jeff Batzli
Designer: Devorah Levinrad
Photography Editor: Christopher Bain
Photo Researcher: Daniella Jo Nilva
Production: Karen L. Greenberg

Typeset by EAC/Interface
Color separations by United South Sea Graphic Art Co., Ltd.
Printed and bound in Hong Kong by Leefung-Asco Printers Ltd.

8 7 6 5 4 3 2 1

To James Madar,
whose love of knowledge
inspires my own.

Acknowledgments

The people with whom I came into contact during the writing of this book helped me understand a number of subjects presented in it. I must thank Diane Freburg for many insights into why crystals work as they do. Genevieve Phelan, Frank Allen, and the late Frank Neubecker provided an enormous body of information and support when dealing with the spiritual matters discussed here. My good friend and fellow writer Frank Gorin was the source of an endless supply of original thoughts and fresh cups of coffee. Fellow writer Sara Godwin kept both my feet planted firmly on the ground by reminding me again and again to keep it simple. Melissa Schwarz of the Michael Friedman Publishing Group was a supportive project editor. Line editor Louise Quayle reminded me of long-neglected editorial essentials such as the active voice and properly placed modifiers. Finally, my young godson, James Madar, is at just the stage of life when the information and ideas presented here can be the most helpful. Writing this for him made me conscious of how important it is to think of every reader as a loved one.

© Bill Kauntz/Courtesy of Ocus Stanley

Contents

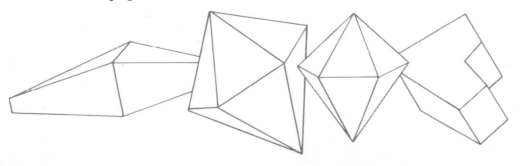

Introduction

The earliest written record of a crystal describes a diamond called Draconitias, a thumbnail-size jewel acquired by a king of Persia for his bride about 1700 B.C. Yet crystals have fascinated humans since long before the impressive Draconitias gem.

The oldest known amulets using crystals date back twenty thousand years. The world's oldest gemstone mine, in Baluchistan, Afghanistan, has been worked continuously for seven thousand years; it supplied the beautiful blue lapis lazuli used to make the famous Egyptian funerary masks such as Tutankhamen's.

TUTANKHAMEN'S COFFIN MASK IS AN EXAMPLE OF THE EXQUISITE JEWELRY CREATED IN ANCIENT EGYPT. THE BLUE LAPIS LAZULI INLAYS WERE CRAFTED BY SLOWLY GRINDING THE STONES AGAINST EACH OTHER BY HAND, USING SAND AS AN ABRASIVE. THE GOLD WAS CAST INTO A MOLD, WORKED INTO SHAPE WITH SHARP METAL TOOLS, THEN POLISHED WITH ANIMAL SKINS AND FUR.

© Scala/Art Resource

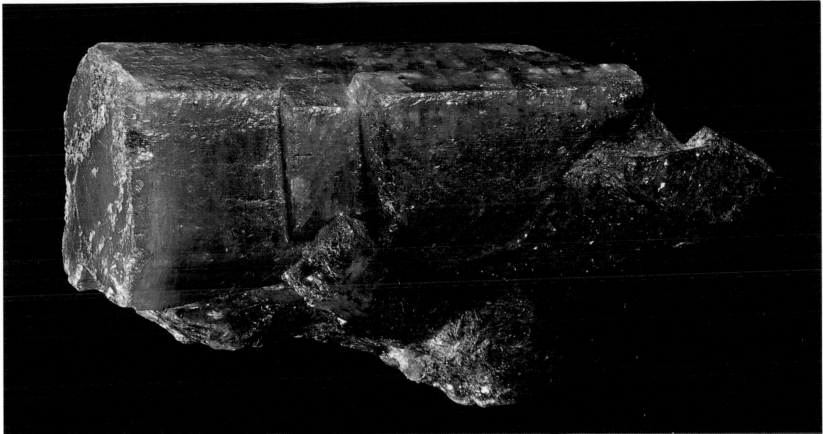

© H. Janson/FPG International

EMERALD IS THE RAREST OF ALL THE FINE GEMSTONES AND HAS ALWAYS BEEN ENDOWED WITH MYSTICAL POWERS. ITS UNIQUE GREEN COLOR COMES FROM TRACE AMOUNTS OF BERYLLIUM.

Crystals have always possessed an aura of mystery. The first crystal jewelry—made of amethyst, quartz, garnet, jade, jasper, lapis lazuli, and emerald—were talismans of tremendous power. Crystals have been used to ward off evil spirits, protect against ghosts, invoke the help of saints or holy persons, keep husbands faithful, guide lost sailors to shore, and influence people in power.

Until the Scientific Revolution in the eighteenth century many people believed crystals contained healing powers that could be tapped in three ways. First, a crystal in a sick person's room focused the invisible energies of spiritual beings and thus effected a cure. A healing crystal could also be placed on or near the afflicted part of the body with this same principle in mind. Finally, crystals were administered in powdered form and eaten—although this could be hazardous, since certain crystals, such as beryl, are poisonous.

Many books advised which crystal should be employed for a particular effect. Few of these suggestions were based on scientific principles. Yet this brings out an important point: The thousands of years of lore about the psychic powers of crystals have received little scientific attention. Though a crystal "cure"

QUARTZ (opposite page) IS THE MOST COMMON CRYSTAL IN THE WORLD. PULVERIZED INTO TINY BITS, QUARTZ BECOMES SAND.

© Bill Kaunitz

HEATED AND FUSED, SAND BECOMES GLASS (above). HERE, LEAD CRYSTALS HAVE BEEN ADDED TO THE GLASS TO CREATE A BRIL- LIANT SPARKLING EFFECT.

might be the result of the placebo effect or a psychosomatic power of suggestion, it might also be true that crystals have properties the scientific establishment hasn't fully discovered. The powers of plants have been much more thoroughly tested than the powers of crystals. In short, we have much to learn.

The mystical lore of crystals can be traced through three periods in Western history over the last thousand years. First, nobles and soldiers returning from the Crusades brought back a mystical wisdom— astrology—that relied on the symbols of the heavens. Three centuries later, during the Renaissance, scholars focused on the observations of the ancient Greeks. The idea developed that certain natural objects, such as birthstones, linked astrological events with human behavior. Birthstones worn on the body were thought to protect a person born under the stone's zodiacal sign. Though over time some ideas about the effect of particular stones have changed, there remained the fundamental principle that a power emanating from the planets and stars affects the way we behave.

Later, the Scientific Revolution explained crystals in terms of atomic structure. Scientists discovered that all matter is composed of waves of energy much like light or radio waves. With this discovery, scientists learned that crystals can vibrate with energy at different frequencies. Glass (a form of crystal) is used in camera and telescope lenses to focus light. Other crystals are used to transmit energy—for example, the quartz crystals used in radios. If all matter is energy, the reasoning goes, then perhaps crystals transmit energy for the human body also.

At one time scientists believed that crystals were nothing more than intricate lattices of atoms and electrons. Today's scientists are grappling with unsettling ideas like the chaos theory to explain why, even in the best of circumstances, things don't always work the way they should. Some New Age thinkers link these scientific theories with the power of crystals, adding yet another dimension to our understanding of the power of these mysterious rocks.

© Bill Kaunitz/Courtesy of Ocus Stanley

THE AMOUNT OF COLOR IN SMOKY QUARTZ (left) DEPENDS ON THE AMOUNT OF IRON OXIDE IN THE CRYSTAL.

© Breck P. Kent

THE BEAUTIFUL ORANGE COLOR OF THIS WOLFRAMITE CRYSTAL COMES FROM THE INTER-PLAY OF LIGHT ON ITS ATOMS OF IRON, MANGANESE, AND TUNGSTEN. "WOLFRAM" IS AN OLD GERMAN NAME FOR TUNGSTEN.

No interpretation of the power of crystals is the "right" one. This book explores the scientific understanding of crystals and their myriad uses in science and industry. It also looks at the metaphysical power attributed to crystals, and at the intricate relationship between physics and metaphysics. Scientists and New Age thinkers both recognize that the ultimate explanation of the universe is basically mystical: We still don't know why it exists. The various interpretations of crystals demonstrate that, although they speak different languages, science and metaphysics both address many of the same concerns.

We might think of crystals as we do the stained glass windows in a great cathedral. They are vividly colored and they inspire awe and feelings of spirituality. Most everyone observing them has the sense that somehow they are better by having experienced such beauty.

The light passing through a stained glass window falls on the stone floor of the cathedral, where passersby gaze and marvel at it. The scientist longs for an understanding of how the phenomena depicted in the light falling on the floor came to be. The metaphysician seeks to explain the meaning of the images depicted high up in the clerestory. Each in his own way finds meaning there.

Crystals are much like stained glass windows. Scientists note their utility—crystals have provided humankind with enormous technological benefits. Yet metaphysicians note that for thousands of years people have attributed to crystals powers beyond the everyday. Today many people think crystals transmit a spiritual or metaphysical energy in much the same way that stained glass windows transmit the physical energy called light.

This book explores these and many other ideas that have developed about crystals. It also examines the practical and useful ways in which crystals affect our lives. In the process, *Crystals* describes one of the most fascinating artifacts humankind has come to know.

PART ONE

The Science of

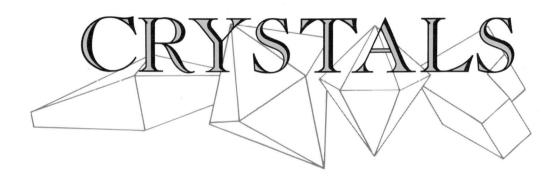

CRYSTALS

(clockwise from top left): © Bill Kaunitz/Courtesy Pappy & Rosa Mae Gossage. © Bill Kaunitz. © Bill Kaunitz/Courtesy of Jim Coleman

1

Clear Ice or Melted Stone?

IT IS FASCINATING TO IMAGINE HOW ANCIENT PEOPLE REACTED WHEN THEY CAME UPON MAGNIFICENT CRYSTAL DEPOSITS LIKE THIS ONE. WE KNOW THIS BLEND OF PINK, WHITE, AND BLACK AS CHABAZITE, BUT TO EARLY WANDERING TRIBES IT MUST HAVE SEEMED A GIFT FROM A DEITY.

Probably no other natural object has generated as many scientific and philosophical theories as the crystal.

Today we know that crystals are composed of geometrically arranged atoms. Some crystals are so small they can be seen only with a microscope. Others are truly gigantic: The largest crystal ever found had to be taken away from its mine on two railroad flatcars. And crystals appear in the oddest places: Mud may simply look like mud, but when magnified in a microscope mud is a vast array of marvelously colored crystals.

While science today explains the crystal in atomic terms, our understanding of how they form and their technological applications has undergone many changes over history.

Crystals and Early Humankind

The completeness of our scientific understanding of crystals is a fairly recent development. But this understanding has roots far back in human experience. More than twenty thousand years ago humans had already acquired considerable technical skills, which they used to paint beautiful images in the caves of Lascaux, Altamira, Padirac, and other places.

These skills testify to a long apprenticeship. No one knows how long it took early artists to develop their understanding of how to crush crystals and muds into pigments and to mix these with tallows and oils to make paint. Though their ultimate goal was to depict the beautiful animals in their world, not necessarily to analyze crystal properties for the pure sake of knowledge, their methods of discovery must have in many ways resembled modern experimental science.

Cave paintings are one art form; adorning the human body is another. Today's vast array of rings, charms, good-luck pieces, crowns, tiaras, cameos, and class rings reflect a long history of discovery. The oldest known jewelry comes from twenty-thousand-year-old graves. We can only guess what special role ancient bits of bone and crystal may have played, but primitive jewelry reveals a mastery of materials that

© Breck P. Kent

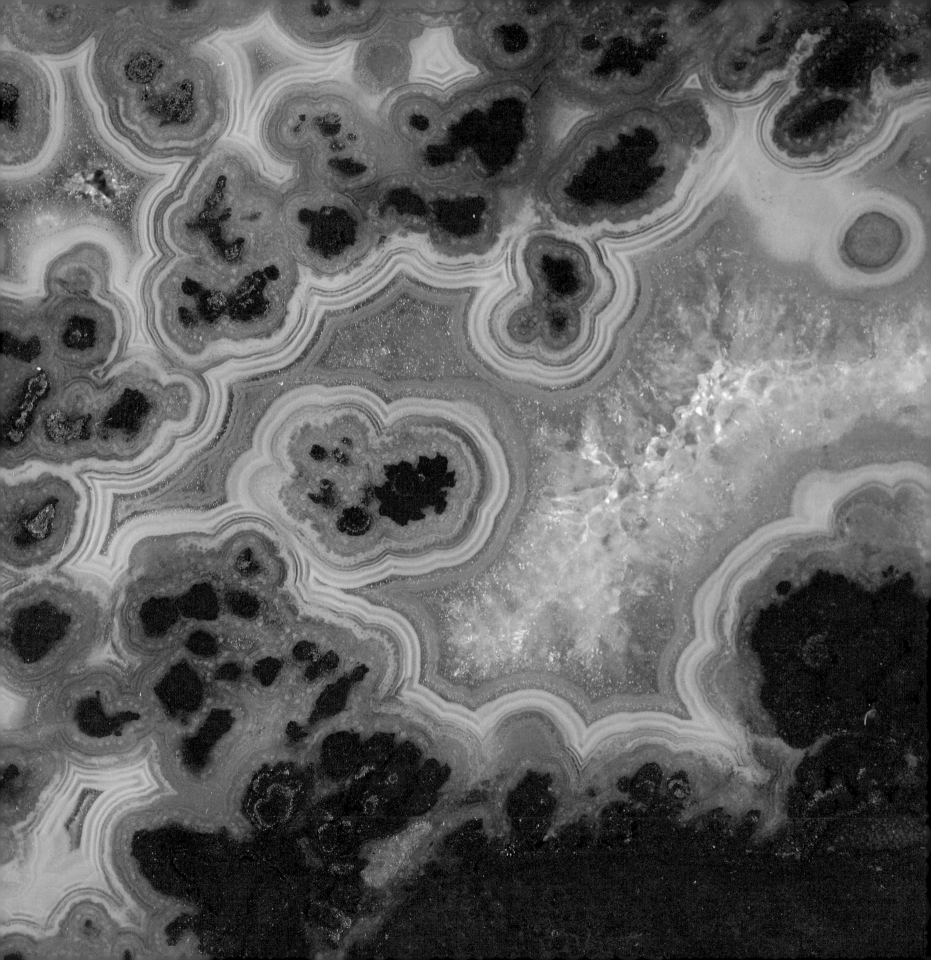

AGATE (left) HAS BEEN USED AS A JEWEL SINCE BEFORE WRITTEN HISTORY. THIS PIECE IS MIXED WITH RED JASPER IN A PATTERN KNOWN AS "CRAZY LACE."

© Scala/Art Resource

CARVED FROM AGATE, THIS CAMEO PORTRAIT OF THE RENAISSANCE DESPOT LUDOVICO IL MORO EMBODIES ONE OF THE HALLMARKS OF A FINE CAMEO—THE QUALITY OF THE CARVING IS SO GOOD IT LOOKS EVEN BETTER MAGNIFIED THAN IT DOES WITH THE NAKED EYE.

indicates an intimate knowledge of fabrication and resources. Such jewelry was probably crafted to adorn, to beautify, to protect the wearer from the misfortunes of the world, and to proclaim the wearer's power and status. For example, we know that Peking man made jewelry from quartz and that Australian aboriginals used amethyst totems in rain-making rites.

As human societies evolved from clan to tribe to state to nation, so did their use of scientific experiment and discovery. Jewelry evolved as well, from amulet to talisman to jewel to diadem. The talismanic symbolism of the diamonds in the British crown jewels is just as important as the technical craft required to make them.

The first recorded writing on the subject of crystals came from a man named Socatus, a physician in the ancient court of Persia. Socatus described a "wondrous stone called Draconitias", which as far as we know is the earliest description of a diamond. In fact, the stone itself still exists as the Shah Diamond. Left uncut in its original crystalline form, this diamond has been inscribed with the names of at least three of its dynastic owners.

The ancient Greeks used clasps set with crystals and other gems to fasten their long, flowing robes. The Romans were especially interested in agate (the name comes from a river in Sicily where the stone was first discovered) and the Romans devised the cameo to exploit the beauty of stones with many thin layers of color. This complex art form long outlived the Romans who developd it, and today the cameo is still a highly regarded adornment.

Crystals have been found in nearly every part of the world. The gravel beds of Sri Lanka and Myanmar (Burma) have provided diamonds, rubies, spinels, and sapphires for millennia. More than two thousand years ago diamonds were already an important source of revenue for the princes of India. Up to the time of the Spanish conquest of Mexico and South America in the 1500s, the richest sources of emeralds were in Egypt and Habachtal. When the conquistadors took over the fabulous emerald deposits of present-day Colombia, the New World quickly revealed itself as a treasure-trove so vast that Colombian emeralds are being mined and traded to this day. Brazil has provided a superb array of topaz, tourmaline, agate, and chrysoberyl. South Africa has been the preeminent source of diamonds for more than a century, although diamonds are also found in Siberia, Australia, Namibia—and Arkansas. Indeed, the diamonds of Arkansas were a staple of American industry; used as abrasives until the development of manmade diamond abrasives in 1955.

The History of Crystal Science

THE ANCIENT GREEKS CAN BE EXCUSED FOR ERRONEOUSLY CONCLUDING THAT STONES LIKE THIS CLEAR QUARTZ CRYSTAL (COLORED ORANGE BY RUST INCLUSIONS) WERE A FORM OF PERMANENT ICE. THEY BELIEVED THERE WERE ONLY FOUR ELEMENTS—AIR, EARTH, WATER, AND FIRE—AND THE ADDITION OR REMOVAL OF ONE ELEMENT FROM THE OTHERS WAS BELIEVED TO PRODUCE ALL THE PHENOMENA WE KNOW IN NATURE. IN THE CASE OF CRYSTALS, THE GREEKS BELIEVED THAT BOTH FIRE AND WATER WERE DRIVEN OFF IN THE PROCESS OF CRYSTALLIZATION, LEAVING PERMANENTLY FROZEN ICE.

Fabled travelers that they were, the early Greeks found certain stones in the Alps that resembled ice, but did not melt. There is little doubt that the material referred to as *krystallos* by ancient Greek writers was what we today call rock crystal—clear, well-crystallized quartz. Since the quartz specimens they found came mostly from the Alps, they concluded that rock crystal must be ice that had been frozen so hard it would never melt.

Ancient Greece was a hotbed of theories. The atomists of the fourth century B.C.—Leucippus, Democritus, Epicurus, Lucretius, and Aristotle—theorized that all matter consisted of an infinite number of indivisible particles called atoms. These atoms, they said, were the only "reality," and moreover, all

© Bill Kaunitz/Courtesy of Pappy & Mae Gossage

THE GEOLOGIST'S NAME FOR THIS CRYSTAL IS HALITE. WE KNOW IT AS SALT. WHETHER FORMED IN HALF-INCH CRYSTALS LIKE THESE NATURAL STONES OR IN TINY GRAINS ON OUR DINING ROOM TABLES, THE CUBIC STRUCTURE IS THE SAME. HALITE SPECIMENS LIKE THIS ONE MUST BE COATED WITH A PRESERVATIVE TO KEEP OUT MOISTURE. WITHOUT IT, ALL THIS BEAUTY WOULD MELT AWAY AS CERTAINLY AS A GRAIN OF SALT IN YOUR SOUP.

these atoms were identical and homogenous. The shape, order, and arrangement of these atoms accounted for the diversity of all natural objects.

The father of crystallography as a science was Theophrastus, a student of Aristotle who wrote the first treatise on gemstones about 300 B.C. He adapted the atomists' theory to explain the formation of crystals. Crystals were stones whose atoms had tiny "hooks and eyes" that grasped each other in regular geometric patterns. He believed that crystals were, in fact, melted stone that had frozen so solid that it could not be melted again.

Plato (428–348 B.C.) had a different theory. He imagined that nature was made up of powers (or qualities): air, earth, fire, and water. These powers were associated with, and contained within, four fundamental geometric shapes of nature: the pyramidal four-faced tetrahedron, the cube, the eight-faced octahedron, and the twenty-faced icosahedron. Plato explained that these elements were so tiny that they could not be seen, but because they could assemble into more complex shapes by grouping together in series of triangles, they could be the basis of fixed figures. Because so many types of triangles existed—isosceles and equilateral, for example—nature could put together an innumerable series of configurations.

Both these theories could explain the obvious characteristics of most crystals—their flat faces, regular angles, systematic arrangement of geometric forms based on triangles, and so on. While the atomists believed all matter to be homogenous, Plato thought crystals were aggregates of the basic geometric shapes in nature. He describes crystals as follows:

> Of the varieties of earth, the one which has been strained through water becomes a stony substance when the water mixed with it is broken by the mixing. When that happens the water is changed into air, and it rushes up to its own region. But as there is no empty space surrounding it, the rushing air thrusts against the surrounding air, which, being heavy, squeezes hard against the spaces in which it is contained. Earth thrust together by air forms a stone that is not soluble by water. The finer and more transparent the stone, the more homogeneous its particles. The coarser the stone, the coarser its particles.

Aristotle (384–322 B.C.) disagreed with Plato's argument because he believed that nature contained no vacuums (or "voids"). Crystals had to form according to the shape of the space in which they grew. While these two schools of thought almost explain the process of crystal formation, no significant advances in the theory of crystallography occurred for another two thousand years.

Much of the knowledge added to crystallography in those two millennia was purely descriptive. The immense thirty-seven volume *Historia Naturalis* by the Roman scholar Pliny the Elder (A.D. 23–79) is an example. Pliny was the quintessential scholar: He quoted everything except what he observed himself. Most of the vast body of encyclopedic learning he left behind was based on the work of Greek philosophers, modified with his own ideas.

Pliny's work was the basis for scientific investigation through the eighteenth century. But his unquestioning acceptance of conflicting theories and observations led to some hilarious errors that plagued naturalists for centuries. His theory of "pregnant" stones was used to explain crystal formation for more than a thousand years. Theophrastus speculated that certain stones could bear young. Pliny modified this

PLATO'S CONCEPT OF IDEAL ARCHETYPAL FORMS IS AT THE HEART OF THE NEW AGE BELIEF THAT CRYSTALS COMMUNICATE ENERGY TO THEIR OWNERS.

© S.E.F./Art Resource

theory by adding that "eagle stones" could be found in eagles' nests and thus must be required for eagle chicks to hatch. Pliny listed several varieties of eagles said to require eagle stones, plus localities where the phenomenon had been observed. Eagle stones, he proposed, consisted of male and female pairs. The female eggs were a pleasing white inside, and made of a soft, claylike material. The male eggs were red and contained a hard stone in the hollow middle.

The experiments of alchemists, which began at about the same time as the philosophical speculations of the Greeks, also contributed to our understanding of crystals. Like the work of early Greek philosophers, the "science" of alchemy also created misinformation that later would have to be undone.

The first alchemical writings appeared in Alexandria, Egypt, about 200 B.C. Early alchemists attempted to speed up the process of gemstone formation through artificial means. The faster and more efficiently one could separate gold from its ore, for example, the richer the yield. Crystals, these alchemists discovered, would break down when heated to very high temperatures in bellows-driven furnaces. In the process, certain characteristic odors (such as sulfur) were emitted.

By the time of the early Christian era the Romans had improved Alexandrine methods. They discovered how to recover mercury from its sulfide and knew gold had an odd affinity for mercury. The gold released, however, was not entirely pure; it was embedded in a gold-mercury amalgam that was mixed with other, undesirable matter in a substance called *gangue*. The Romans then discovered that by forcing this *gangue* through leather the gold-mercury amalgam would remain, which could then be separated into the two metals by heating it in an alembic, a kind of still.

© Scala/Art Resource

ARISTOTLE WAS A REALIST. HE BELIEVED THAT CRYSTALS FORM BECAUSE THEIR HEAT AND MOISTURE ARE "DRIVEN OUT BY COLD."

SHOWN HERE IN CRYSTAL FORM, SULFUR HAS HAD A MARKED IMPACT ON HISTORY. ANCIENT GREEKS LEARNED TO COMBINE SULPHUR WITH PHOSPHOROUS IN A SUBSTRATE OF ANIMAL LARD TO CREATE A SUBSTANCE THAT WHEN IGNITED, COULDN'T BE PUT OUT. "GREEK FIRE" WAS RESPONSIBLE FOR SEVERAL GREEK MILITARY VICTORIES.

Philosophers tried to explain what the alchemists were discovering. One idea was that mercury embodied a principle of one kind of matter—metallicity—and sulfur embodied another—combustibility. If the principle of metallicity could be enhanced and the principle of combustibility reduced, base metals could be changed into gold.

This idea led experimenters down a false path that endured until the seventeenth century. The Middle Ages is replete with well-intended but incorrect crystallographic lore that is useful mainly because it con-

© Breck P. Kent

ALTHOUGH WE ARE MOST FAMILIAR WITH NATURAL GOLD IN THE FORM OF AMORPHOUS GLOBS, GOLD CAN IN FACT CRYSTALLIZE UNDER THE RIGHT CONDITIONS OF TEMPERATURE AND PRESSURE. ALCHEMISTS THOUGHT THAT THESE FORTUITOUS OCCURRENCES RESULTED FROM MAGICAL PROPERTIES—PROPERTIES THAT, WHEN FULLY UNDERSTOOD, WOULD ENABLE THEM TO TRANSMUTE BASE METALS TO GOLD.

© Breck P. Kent

firms the existence of certain gems. On the whole, medieval experimenters were much more concerned with the magical properties of crystals than with their scientific properties.

Though Marbodus, a bishop of Rennes in France, wrote a treatise on crystals during the eleventh century which suggested that the legendary lore of alchemy be verified by experiments, science as we know it did not address crystals for another five hundred years. Astrological and speculative lore dominated European crystallography until an Antwerp physician named Anselmus De Boot (1573–1639) penned a brief but highly original work called *De Gemmis et Lapidibus* in 1609.

De Boot's work appeared during the Renaissance, a time in which scientific knowledge based on observation was replacing religious dogma. Between the fall of Rome in A.D. 465 and about A.D. 1500, the powerful religious doctrines of the Catholic church slowly replaced primitive animistic and superstitious beliefs such as those of the Druids, who thought that oak groves were abodes of the gods and that races of miniature people called fairies and elves lived beneath the surface of the earth. Scientific discoveries that challenged church doctrine were considered heretical.

By the time of De Boot's work, the church's power was in decline. The Renaissance ushered in an era in which political and intellectual circles accepted systems of thought that did not depend on religious authority.

(Right) ALTHOUGH THEY DON'T LOOK IT, THESE CRYSTALS ARE IN FACT COMMON EVERYDAY QUARTZ. AT SOME POINT IN THEIR FORMATION THEY CAME IN CONTACT WITH IRON OXIDE (RUST) THAT HAD BEEN DISSOLVED IN WATER. THE OXIDE ADHERED TO THE SURFACES OF THE CRYSTALS, IMPARTING THIS BEAUTIFUL LUSTER. ROCK CRYSTAL (far right), WHICH IS A PURE FORM OF QUARTZ, HAS THE PROPERTY OF TRANSMITTING LIGHT WITHOUT CHANGING IT. ITS REFLECTIONS AND ITS REFRACTIONS APPEAR THE SAME. THIS SPECIMEN HAS BEEN ILLUMINATED WITH DIFFERENT COLORED LIGHTS TO ILLUSTRATE THE EFFECT.

In *De Gemmis et Lapidibus* Anselmus De Boot emphasizes the material rather than the magical properties of crystals. He speaks respectfully of older beliefs explaining the properties of crystals, but always returns to scientific explanations. In its own way, his work was the first scientific analysis of crystals. De Boot's book takes its place on the shelf beside Theophrastus, Plato, and Marbodus, whose crystal studies are based more on "science" and less on superstition or metaphysics.

Half a century before De Boot, the German scholar Georg Bauer (1494–1555)—better known by his Latinized name, Agricola—reinterpreted the Platonic-alchemical theory of matter in his work *De Re Metallica* (1530). Agricola assigned the four alchemical qualities of salinity, ignitability, earthiness, and metallicity to the properties of metals and crystals. Agricola's great contribution was the orderliness of his classifications under these four main properties. Like his predecessors, Agricola was fascinated by the regular forms and geometric exactness of crystals; he tried to devise a systematic explanation for them. Though Agricola based much of his theory on incorrect information handed down from earlier writers, his work represents an important contribution to crystallography.

After Agricola, advances in what we now know as the earth sciences developed at a fast pace. De Boot's work inspired the Italian historian Hieronymous (Jerome) Cardanus (1501–1576) to write his own interpretation of crystals in 1563. His speculation centered on the geometry of crystals, attributing their

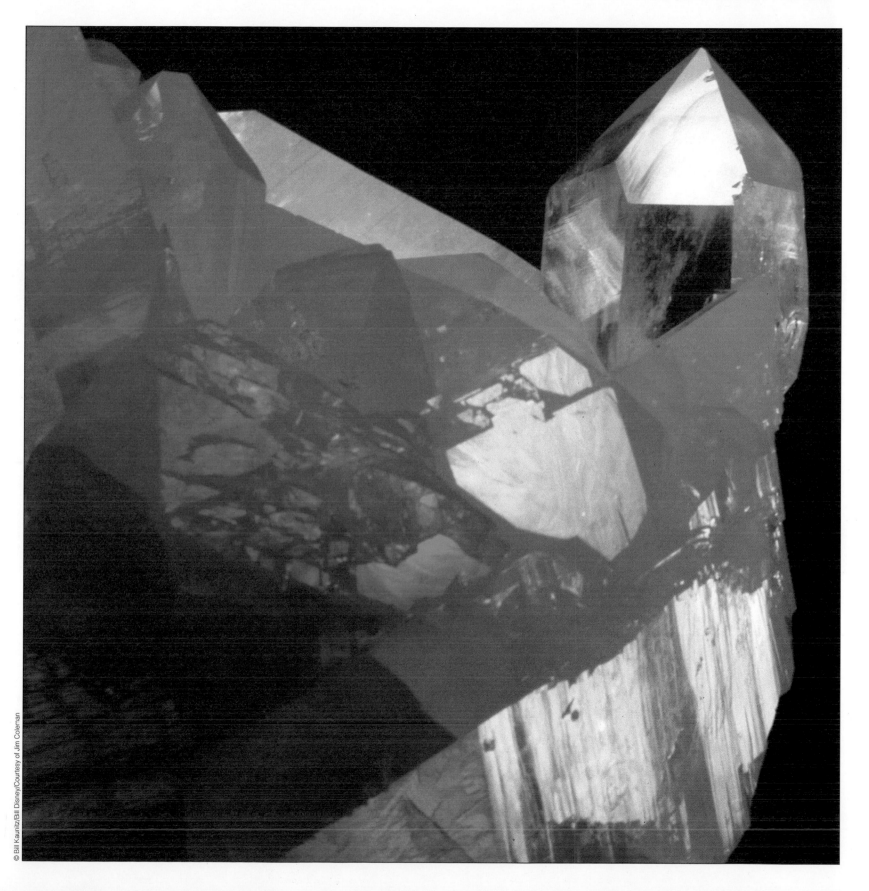

© Bill Kaunitz/Bill Disney/Courtesy of Jim Coleman

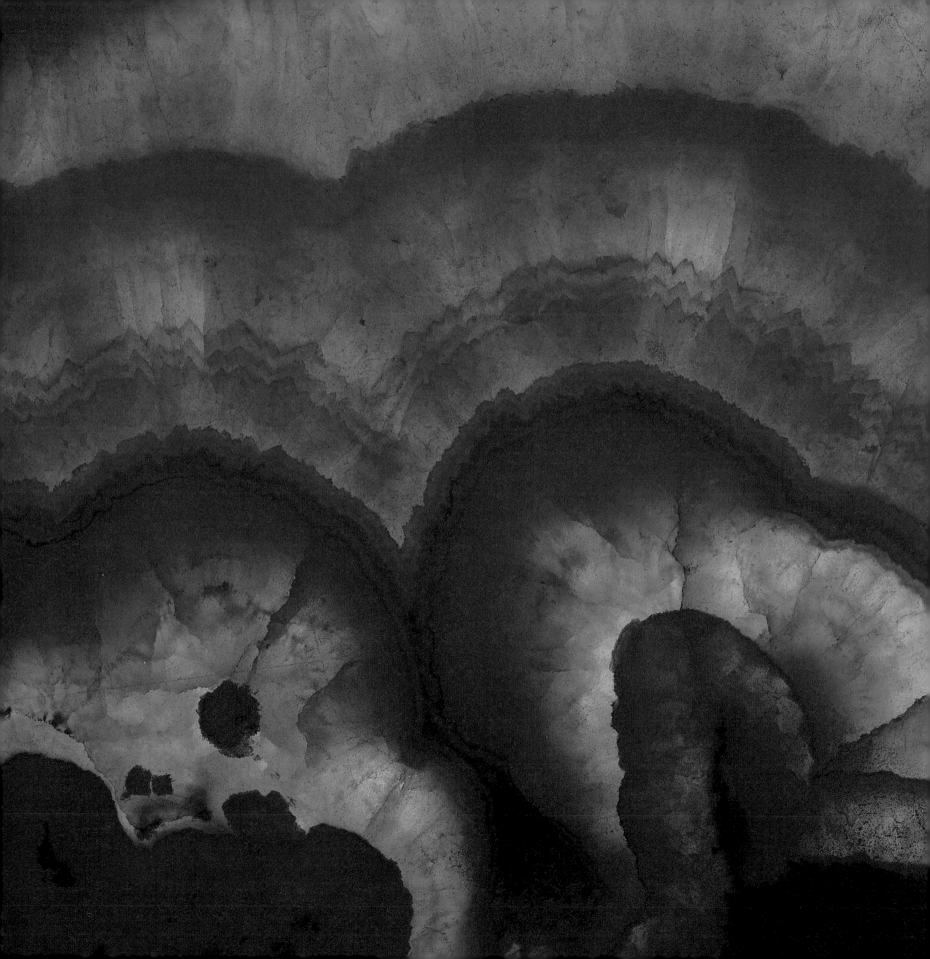

THE SERENE
BEAUTY OF THIS
STONE BELIES A
COMPLEX MAKEUP.
THE BULBOUS
SHAPES ARE
CALLED "BOTRY-
OIDAL" BECAUSE
THEY RESEMBLE
BUNCHES OF
GRAPES (FROM THE
LATIN WORD FOR
GRAPE CLUSTER,
BOTRYS). THE
ROSE-RED COLOR IS
A HALLMARK OF
MANGANESE COM-
POUNDS, IN THIS
CASE MANGANESE
CARBONATE.

shapes to natural forces other than Agricola's alchemical forces. While Cardanus did not draw this conclusion himself, his theory reintroduced the idea that the universe was ordered according to the ancient atomistic principles of Leucippus and Democritus.

In the middle 1600s, the Swiss philosopher Nicholas Steno (1638–1687) advanced crystallography by precisely measuring the various angles at which crystals intersect. His work challenged Platonic thinking by assuming a new set of conditions. Although he was unable to deduce the atomic lattice structure that is the basis of modern crystallography, Steno provided a key concept in our understanding of matter: Natural relationships that result from the interaction of forces occuring under identical conditions yield results that are always the same.

With Steno's theoretical base in place, contemporary crystallography rapidly developed. In 1774, the German scientist Abraham Werner (1736–1789) classified minerals by their properties of color, hardness, and flammability. His work inspired a wave of investigation all over Europe which culminated in the development of the periodic table of the elements, first formulated by the Russian chemist Dmitry Mendeleyev (1834–1907). His periodic table described physical properties for elements that had not yet been isolated. Mendeleyev completed the transition in crystallography from superstition and myth to observed fact and mathematical explanation. Yet even he acknowledged a truth first articulated by Isaac Newton, whose work in physics matched Mendeleyev's in chemistry: "If I have seen further than others, it was because I stood on the shoulders of giants."

The discoveries of modern geology complete our understanding of the formation of crystals. Now we know that Earth's continents constantly move—albeit slowly, over eons—and eventually collide with each other. As they crunch together, some portions are heated to the melting point and then cool over vast expanses of time. As they cool, some elements and molecules congeal at different temperatures than others. This is what creates different crystals. Many crystals and ores occur in seams, pockets of rock that maintained a uniform temperature long enough for elements with specific characteristics to separate out from the others. Yet despite all the variables that create different rocks and crystals, no element has yet formed that wasn't predicted by Mendeleyev.

The historical giants, from Plato and Aristotle to De Boot and Mendeleyev, each made significant contributions to our understanding of how crystals form. Scientists have built upon their work to arrive at our most recent theories regarding the science of crystals.

2

The Modern Perspective

THE PURPLE-
RED COLOR OF
AMETHYST IS A
MYSTERY.
CHEMICALLY,
AMETHYST IS
QUARTZ. BUT THE
MOST EXACT SCIEN-
TIFIC ANALYSIS DOES
NOT EXPLAIN WHAT
IMPURITY GIVES
THE STONE ITS
DEEP COLOR. THE
WORD AMETHYST
COMES FROM
THE ANCIENT
GREEK PHRASE *A
METHYEIN*, WHICH
MEANS "NOT TO BE
DRUNK." LEGEND
HAS IT THAT AN
AMETHYST'S
WINE-LIKE COLOR
BLOCKS THE
EFFECTS OF HAVING
DRUNK TOO MUCH
WINE. HENCE THE
GREEKS EMPLOYED
POWDERED
AMETHYST AS A
HANGOVER CURE.

Today we know that crystals are elaborate arrangements of atoms. Atoms are so small that a crystal the size of a pencil eraser might contain 100 billion billion of them. Small though this is, atoms themselves are an elaborate arrangement of even tinier particles—a nucleus of protons and neutrons surrounded by a spinning cloud of electrons. The way atoms bond to each other is decided mainly by how these whirling electrons react to each other—the way they move from atom to atom (resulting in the production of electricity) and the way they move up and down within their orbits around the nucleus (resulting in the phenomenon of light and other types of radiation).

Since there are ninety-two naturally occurring elements, each with a different-shaped nucleus and cloud of orbiting electrons, it is no surprise that the interaction of these elements is extraordinarily complex and varied. For example, there are more than 2,500 naturally occurring crystals, which are made from twenty-five of the ninety-two elements.

When atoms assemble to make a compound, the visible result is determined by the way the compound's atoms have arranged themselves. This is largely determined by the shells of electrons surrounding each atom. The word shell is used to describe an energy level at which a given number of electrons can whirl around a nucleus in a stable manner. There can be many shells of electrons around an atom, each holding a specific number of electrons.

When energy from outside—for example, light, heat, the movement of nearby electrons, and so on—strikes an electron shell, its electrons move to the next higher shell. They stay there until the surrounding energy is reduced; then the electrons move to a lower shell, giving off the extra energy accumulated in the process. Often this extra energy is in the form of light. The particular wavelength of this light—and its color—depends on the energy released by the electrons. The way light of a certain wavelength strikes the eye triggers the perception of color.

The first things we notice about crystals are their regular geometric shape and their color. The geometric shapes occur because the atoms in crystals bond together in very regular formations called

© Bill Kaunitz

lattices when crystals congeal from liquid to solid. We see their color when external energy (light) enters the crystal, excites its orbiting electrons into a higher shell, and then leaves. The electrons in the crystal absorb some of the light's energy, and reflect it back to us. This is what our eye interprets as color.

Certain elements, such as chromium, titanium, boron, zirconium, beryllium, tungsten, and uranium, are very important in the composition of crystals because in trace quantities they impart the beautiful colors and structures that we associate with fine gems. For example, sapphire and ruby, which are mostly aluminum oxide, have a nearly identical chemical composition. When aluminum oxide is perfectly pure it

© Bill Kaunitz/Courtesy of Lawrence Stoller

"INCLUSIONS" ARE FOREIGN BODIES THAT HAVE BEEN TRAPPED IN A CRYSTAL AS IT CONGEALS FROM ITS MOLTEN STATE. THESE CAN BE A GAS, LIQUID, OR SOLID THAT DID NOT RESPOND TO THE SAME PRESSURES AND TEMPERATURES THAT CAUSED THE CRYSTAL TO FORM. THIS CLEAR QUARTZ CRYSTAL HAS INCLUSIONS OF SILICA, CHLORITE, AND IRON.

is colorless. But if a trace of chromium is present, it produces the color ruby. If traces of iron and titanium are present, aluminum oxide shows up as sapphire blue. The total amount of these infinitesmal impurities can be in the thousandths of a percent of the crystal's total makeup.

Crystals Began with the Universe

The complex story of the earth's crystals began long before the earth itself existed. During the late nineteenth century, astronomers puzzled over wispy objects in the night sky that looked like clouds—nebulas they called them, after the Latin word for clouds. Were these nebulas in our own Milky Way galaxy or outside our galaxy. With the development of the telescope (based on the crystal glass) and photography (based on the crystal silver halide) early in the twentieth century, astronomers discovered that many nebulas were in fact remote galaxies filled with billions of stars very much like our own. Some of these stars ended their days peacefully like slowly dying embers (as will our Sun). Others exploded into a brilliance so stupefying that they briefly outshone their billions of neighbors to become the brightest single object in the universe.

Over the years astronomers discovered that these exploding stars—called supernovas—blew into space enormous quantities of the same elements from which the earth was made. In fact, the process that matured the stars created the elements of the earth. Scientists estimate that the universe of galaxies is now about 15 billion years old and the earth and solar system a little over 4 billion years old. Between the beginning of the universe and the beginning of Earth so many stars exploded that more than enough material was available to make our earth—and perhaps many other planets as well. This material gathered into gigantic clouds of dust and gas that dot the galaxies like pepper in soup. Our solar system condensed out of these clouds.

As our earth coalesced out of the "local" cloud, the heavier elements fell toward the center first. One of the most abundant elements blown from a supernova is iron, and iron, being a heavy element, forms most of the core of the earth. All the known elements are found in the earth's crust and atmosphere, although sometimes in minuscule quantities.

The early Earth was an uninviting habitat: A thin crust, riven by fissures and volcanoes, had formed as the molten ball of elements cooled. Over unimaginable spans of time the continents thickened out of this

© Bill Kaunitz/Courtesy of Lawrence Stoller

SOME CRYSTALS CONTAIN OTHER CRYSTALS INSIDE THEM. RUTILE IS A TITANIUM DIOXIDE COMPOUND THAT OFTEN CONTAINS A SMALL AMOUNT OF IRON. IT CRYSTALLIZES UNDER DIFFERENT TEMPERATURE AND PRESSURE CONDITIONS THAN QUARTZ, FORMING THE INCLUSIONS SEEN HERE.

crust and the ocean basins formed, eventually filling with water. Because the continents floated on a thick layer of molten rock (magma), they slowly moved across the earth's surface, pushed by rising plumes of hotter magma spreading away from where it rose beneath the oceans. The complete theory of this process, called "plate tectonics," developed only in the last twenty years.

Crystals began to appear on Earth as the original molten ball cooled. The composition of the original ball was not uniform, much in the same way a bowl of soup is not uniform. Pockets of chemical compounds that collected and formed under specific heat and pressure conditions became crystals and metallic ores as they cooled. Later, as the continents formed and began to slide into each other, more crystals were formed as the pressure of the land masses' collisions remelted the earth's original crystal materials. Today the earth's crust is an enormously complex place, and it is no surprise that it is characterized by crystals of a great many colors, shapes, and chemical compositions.

© Bill Kaunitz/Courtesy of L Lawrence Stoller

A CLOSER EXAMINATION OF THE SAME RUTILE'S BRILLIANT RED-BROWN LUSTER REVEALS THAT THIS UNIQUE COLOR IS ITSELF MADE OF TINY TOUCHES OF ORANGE, GREEN, AND BLUE THAT BLEND TOGETHER.

When humans began to walk the face of the earth, they found crystals in rock formations and stream-beds. These strange and beautiful objects were first regarded as healing and religious agents. In our own scientifically oriented time, crystals are acknowledged as one of nature's most perfect models of the arrangement of matter—and perhaps of the way the universe is structured.

A Beautiful World of Diversity

Many crystals are so small that a microscope is necessary to view them. Often even a magnifying glass will reveal glints and flashes of color that indicate countless crystals of many different kinds in a substance the ordinary eye perceives as a solid mass.

Early scientists puzzled over the fact that while most crystals are quite small, some grow to gigantic size. One crystal of the rare mineral beryl, discovered in Madagascar, weighed forty tons (36 metric tons). In

Ontario, Canada, a mica crystal weighing sixty tons (54 metric tons) measured thirty-three feet long and fourteen feet across (10 × 4 m). From experiments, scientists eventually concluded that size usually depends on the length of time and the space a crystal has when its molten minerals originally cool. (See page 52 for instructions on making your own crystals.)

However, other crystal curiosities were less easy to explain. For example, why are certain crystals, such as quartz, found in most parts of the world, while others appear in only a few places? A case in point is a crystal called Benitoite, which occurs only on a few acres in San Benito County, California, and nowhere else in the world. Before the discovery of bauxite, the sole source of aluminum ore in the entire world was a cryolite deposit in Greenland that weighed millions of tons; the only other known cryolite deposits never amounted to more than a few pounds.

Uneven and spotty crystal and mineral deposits around the world piqued early geologists' curiosity. Why weren't the earth's minerals found everywhere? Exploring this question helped scientists learn about the makeup of the earth's interior. The scientists found that patterns of certain mineral deposits could be predicted. Gold, being heavy, would slowly sink in streambeds after it had been dislodged from its original stone. (A set of German prints from the fifteenth century shows miners pushing hollow reeds into sandy pools, capping the reeds with their hands, drawing them out of the water with the sand trapped inside, then depositing the sand in placer pans for washing.)

From astronomers geologists learned that the moon orbits unevenly around the earth. This implied that the earth had an average density much greater than the density of most minerals—about five and one-half times the density of water, which is about twice the density of most minerals. Geologists theorized that the earth's interior must be very heavy.

Over the years geologists collected evidence from such disparate sources as volcanism, earthquake patterns, astronomy, chemistry, magnetism, meteorites, mineshafts, and drill holes, and deduced that the earth consists of many layers. These layers grow increasingly hot and dense toward the earth's core. Geologists attribute the earth's mass and density to a huge amount of iron concentrated below the surface and reaching all the way to its center.

This hot, heavy mass at Earth's center creates nearly all the geological phenomena that occur on its surface. As anyone who has watched a pan of soup simmering on a stove realizes, heat wells upward and concentrates certain components—i.e., the rice seems always to gather in a layer near the bottom, green

QUARTZ IS NOT ONLY ONE OF THE PRETTIEST CRYSTALS IN THE WORLD, IT IS ALSO THE MOST ABUNDANT. AS THE MOLTEN BALL OF THE PROTO-EARTH SLOWLY COOLED AFTER ITS FORMATION, THE HEAVIEST ELEMENTS—MAINLY IRON—SETTLED INTO THE CENTRAL CORE. SILICON AND OXYGEN, TWO OF THE LIGHTER ELEMENTS, FLOATED ON THE SURFACE, AND WHEN THEY COMBINED THEY MADE QUARTZ. THE QUARTZ CRYSTALS WERE THEN WORN BY WIND AND WATER INTO SAND.

peppers in another layer partway up, tomatoes a little higher, and spices on top. Heavier elements concentrate in the middle of the pan with the thinner liquid around the edges. The only way to alter this process is to change the heat.

The earth, of course, can't turn off its internal heat, so it continues to seethe in an immense slow boil. The continents on the surface literally float on a hot molten broth of iron and other heavy elements. As the continents slowly career and crunch into one another, they raise mountain ranges, create volcanos, change the course of rivers, elevate seabeds into high mountain plains—and concentrate minerals into certain zones more densely than elsewhere.

© Bill Kaunitz/Courtesy of Bob Bailey & Gary Anderson

© Breck P. Kent

TOURMALINE (below) IS OFTEN USED BY JEWELRY MAKERS IN ITS NATURAL STATE. (Right) QUARTZ CRYSTALS STILL EMBEDDED IN ROCK.

Baked in the Earth's Oven

Today scientists know that crystals owe their appearance and composition to the temperatures and pressures that existed deep in the earth at the time when the crystals formed. Timing also plays an important role, since certain crystals, such as diamonds, require a very long "bake" in the earth's oven.

Certain atoms have an affinity for one another. Silicon and oxygen, for example, bond so readily that the resulting compound, silicon dioxide (which in its crystallized form is known as quartz) is the most abundant on earth—in fact, 99 percent of all the dust blowing on the earth's winds is made of tiny particles of quartz. Silicon is a basic building block of many crystals, including emerald, aquamarine, tourmaline, topaz, zircon, peridot, and garnet. For this reason, these and many other crystals, are called silicates. Other crystals, notably ruby, sapphire, and spinel, are formed in large part from oxygen in combination with other elements. These are called "oxides".

These basic elements form the earth's various rocks and minerals by one of three processes. *Igneous* rocks solidify after cooling from a very hot, molten state. *Sedimentary* rocks build up from deposits of materials such as sand and animal shells, which are compressed into stone by the weight of the earth. *Metamorphic* rocks form when heat, pressure, or chemical action change a rock with one set of characteristics into rock with very different characteristics—for example, soft limestone converts into hard marble when it is heated and compressed at the same time.

Crystals form when changing temperatures beneath the earth's surface first melt a mass of molecules and atoms, then cool them slowly. As they cool, the atoms arrange themselves in symmetrical lattices. The crystal's form is really a simple molecular structure on a grand scale. They take shape according to the way in which their atoms combine. These atoms create regular geometric patterns because they always align themselves in the same way at a given temperature. Quartz, for example, repeats over and over the same pattern of two atoms of silicon attached to one atom of silicon.

© Bill Kaunitz/Courtesy of Gary Fleck

How Crystals Form

Many rocks are crystalline; they consist of countless microscopic crystals formed when one or many different kinds of minerals are thrown together into a solid mass. You can see the crystals in granite easily with the unaided eye. However, the crystals in most rocks are so small that a microscope is needed to see them. A type of limestone called travertine forms from calcium carbonate crystals precipitated from ground water. The pressure and heat of the earth turns this fine-grained travertine into a coarser grained but tougher marble.

Gem crystals occur in only a tiny fraction of the earth's crust. Valued for their color, luster, transparency, and rarity, gems form when their chemical components transmute, solidify, clarify, and finally reach the earth's surface. This complex, time-consuming, and circuitous route can, from the time the chemicals first combine to the moment a gem finally surfaces, span millions of years.

Some crystals form far beneath the subcontinental lakes of lava that make up the earth's mantle. The 1,700-mile (2720 km) thick mantle extends from about 20 miles (32 km) beneath the continents to the earth's molten-iron core. Diamonds, for example, require temperatures above 1,200 degrees centigrade and pressures typical of depths of 150 miles (240 km) below the earth's surface to form. Just above the diamond-forming region, between the mantle and the earth's crust, ultrabasic rocks form pools of gem-quality peridot.

Most gemstones are carried to the earth's surface by upwelling magma or during periods of mountain building. The rubies and spinels of Burma reach the surface in this way. Formed in immense heat and pressure beneath the Himalayan mountains, they slowly rise to the surface, where, with the effects of weather, they break loose and are swept along down streams and rivers. Denser and heavier than other river gravels, these gems tend to accumulate in slow eddies and shallows, where they form

THE BEST LAPIS (below) IS DARK BLUE AND FLECKED WITH PYRITE, WHICH GLITTERS LIKE GOLD. LESSOR LAPIS IS STREAKED WITH GRAY BANDS. IF THERE ARE NO FLECKS OR BANDS, BUT THE STONE HAS BITS OF WHITE IN IT, IT ISN'T LAPIS AT ALL BUT RATHER SODALITE, WHICH IS OFTEN PASSED OFF AS LAPIS BY JEWELRY MAKERS.

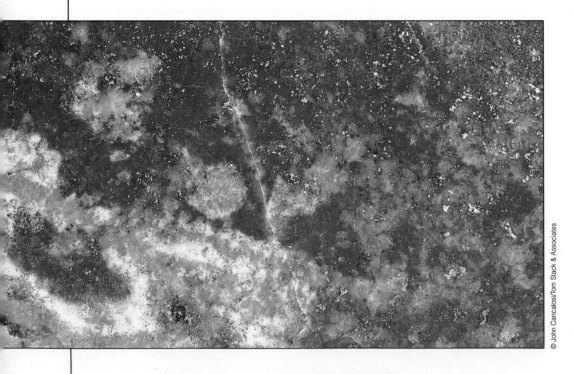

© John Cancalosi/Tom Stack & Associates

© Breck P. Kent

THE KNOBS ON THIS DEPOSIT OF MALACHITE AND AZURITE FORMED SLOWLY OUT OF A WATER-BASED SOLUTION. SOME MINERALS DISSOLVE IN WATER, AND THEN WHEN CONDITIONS ARE RIGHT, THE WATER EVAPORATES. AS A NEW SOLUTION REPLACES WHAT HAS EVAPORATED, MORE LAYERS ARE ADDED.

alluvial deposits that have been mined for thousands of years.

The same is true for the zircons, garnets, rubies, and sapphires that congealed in the basalt lavas of Thailand. Once the gems arrive at the surface, rain and wind break down the cobblelike stone in which they are embedded. Finally, the stones accumulate in river sands.

Shallower—though still searing hot— molten magmas convert the simple alumi- nious shales often found in the earth's upper crust into slate that contains garnet and other gems. And magma rising toward the earth's surface interacts with limestone to form lapis lazuli.

Some crystals contain high concen- trations of rare elements—such as lithium, beryllium, or boron—because the molten liquid concentrates over time and the resid- ual elements precipitate out. Also, some elements crystallize at specific temperatures, thereby concentrating elements which crys- tallize at lower temperatures.

Near the earth's surface, upwelling magma begins to interact with groundwater. Water is a powerful solvent. Many elements easily dissolve in water and are carried to locations far from their origins. Crystals such as malachite and azurite, both copper carbonates, form when water carries them far from their original ores.

Quartz and chalcedony are concentrated in fissures from liquids rich in silica. Most amethyst is found in spherical cavities that occur when the gases in lava seep away, leaving a mineral-rich chamber.

Other crystalline gems form over great spans of time. Opals are an extraordinarily complex assemblage of tiny bits of silica that cool so slowly that they do not separate into chemical components. This is why opal's glittering array of colored "chips" is embed- ded in a liquid with neither bubbles nor the characteristic cleavage lines of crystals.

ALTHOUGH THIS QUARTZ CRYSTAL HAS BEEN CARVED INTO A SPHERE, IT IS THE SAME CRYSTALLINE SUBSTANCE AS A PIECE OF QUARTZ FRESHLY TAKEN FROM THE EARTH. IN THIS BALL, SPIDERY FILAMENTS OF RUTILE GIVE AN UNUSUAL BEAUTY TO THE IMAGES REFRACTED WITHIN IT.

Identifying Crystals

The faces of crystals are flat and smooth because their atoms combine in three-dimensional lattices of fixed rows and spaces. Although the eye can't see the atoms, when X rays pass through a crystal they reveal the atoms' pattern. Even if a quartz crystal is shaped into a sphere, the atomic pattern reflected in X rays remains constant, like a human finger print.

The growth patterns of crystals also distinguish them from other minerals. Crystals can only add layer upon layer of their own substance to the outside; they may get bigger, but they don't evolve into something else. All crystals form in one of seven different shapes (see The Structure of Crystals, page 44). Most metals, in contrast, take the shape of whatever cavity or seam their original mass occupied when it cooled from liquid to solid. (However, many metals do in fact crystallize and behave like crystals under certain conditions.)

Yet the rules that govern the atomic lattices that characterize most crystals can be broken occasionally. Some crystals that appear quite unalike are in fact almost identical. Obsidian, for example, is a familiar sleek, black rock; primitive hunters all over the world preferred it above all other stones in the making of spear points and arrowheads. Granite, a common decorative facing on the outside of many office buildings, is also familiar. Despite their drastically different outward appearances, obsidian and granite are chemically almost identical. Both are silicates that contain almost exactly the same elements in almost exactly the same amounts.

Obsidian and granite are different because of where and how they form. Obsidian results when red-hot magma cools so quickly its atoms don't have time to arrange themselves into the regular geometric shapes of most crystals; the result is an amorphous glassy substance that breaks along sharp, ragged edges. Obsidian is considered a crystal because X ray diffraction shows the orderly arrangement of its atoms—just as an X ray reveals the crystalline orderliness of a crystal ball.

Granite, on the other hand, develops deep in the earth where the cooling process is slow enough to permit crystals to form along lattice lines favored by its various atoms. Granite's characteristic mottled appearance results from its many different minerals, each crystallized into its own unique pattern—some cloudy, some clear, and many others brilliantly colored. When granite is broken, it cracks along the borders of its crystals, not across the middle of them. Obsidian breaks in conchoidal waves (from the Latin for "like a shell") that radiate away from the impact point.

© Bill Kaunitz

© Allen B. Smith/Tom Stack & Associates

The Structure of Crystals

CRYSTALS FORMED FROM SILICATE COMPOUNDS ARE OFTEN HEXAGONAL. QUARTZ (right) IS THE BEST-KNOWN EXAMPLE, BUT THERE ARE MANY OTHERS AS WELL.

Long ago scientists noticed that nearly all crystals with the same makeup had the same shape too. All crystals can take one of seven basic crystal shapes. In addition to color, hardness, and other identifying features, a crystal can be identified by the axes within it and the angles at which these axes intersect.

Isometric crystals are cube-shaped. All three axes have the same length and all intersect at right angles. Salt is the best-known isometric crystal.

Tetragonal crystals also intersect at right angles, but only two faces are of the same length; the others are longer. Four-sided prisms and pyramids are examples.

Hexagonal crystals have four axes. Three intersect at 60-degree angles and are of the same length. The fourth is at a 90-degree angle to the others.

Trigonal crystals are much like hexagonal crystals, except that in hexagonal crystals a cross-section of the base has six sides, whereas in the trigonal system a cross-section of the base has only three sides.

Orthorhombic, or lozenge-shaped, crystals have three axes that intersect at right angles, but the three axes are all of different lengths.

Monoclinic (singly inclined) crystals have three axes of two different lengths. Two of the axes are at right angles to each other, while the third is inclined (veers off at an unusual angle).

Triclinic (thrice inclined) crystals have three axes of different lengths that are also inclined toward each other. A typical example is a crystal with paired faces.

Most crystals are not as perfectly formed as these ideal examples. Some crystals have faces that are more pronounced than others, but it is always the sequence of angles between the faces that identifies a crystal type. Sometimes, because of their complex chemical makeup, certain crystals exhibit features of two or more systems; for example,

WHEN AMETHYST FORMS ON THE SIDE OF A DRUSE (right), THE PUREST PART OF THE LIQUID SILICON OXIDE CONDENSES ON A "SEED"—A PORTION OF THE DRUSE WALL THAT COOLS THE LIQUID UNTIL IT BEGINS TO CRYSTALIZE. AS THE CRYSTAL SLOWLY GROWS AWAY FROM THE DRUSE WALL, THE TRACE ELEMENTS WHICH GIVE AMETHYST ITS BEAUTIFUL COLOR BECOME MORE CONCENTRATED TOWARDS THE TIP, WHICH IS WHY THE CRYSTALS ARE SMALLER AND WHITER NEAR THE WALLS AND SO VIVID IN THE MIDDLE.

there are eighty known varieties of calcite, which combine various crystal shapes.

Sometimes crystals are found in highly unusual forms called pseudomorphs. These generally occur when an uncrystallized liquid occupies the space vacated by a dissolved mineral; or, sometimes, the liquid forms a crust around an existing crystal.

A special—and strikingly beautiful—form of crystal is the druse. Druses are formed on the walls of hollows left in rock when pockets of hot magmatic gas cools. The cooling gas leaves a void, later filled by a liquid that condenses on the walls to form geodes. Amethyst geodes are the best known druses.

© Brack P. Kent

GYPSUM (below) IS SO SOFT IT CAN BE SCRATCHED BY A FINGERNAIL. SPECIMENS LIKE THIS MUST BE HANDLED WITH GREAT CARE. ONE REASON FOR GYPSUM'S SOFT-NESS IS THAT ITS CALCIUM SULFATE MOLECULES ARE "HYDROUS", WHICH MEANS INTERFACED WITH WATER. THE WATER MAKES FOR POOR BONDS BETWEEN THE MOLECULES THAT CAN BE BROKEN DOWN EVEN BY LIGHT PRESSURE WITH A FINGER. FLUORITE (opposite page) IS MADE OF CALCIUM. IT COMES IN A VARIETY OF COLORS. ITS SHAPE (THE EIGHT-SIDED OCTOHEDRON), ITS HARDNESS (MOHS 4), AND ITS CLEAVAGE ARE WHAT DISTIN-GUISH IT FROM OTHER CRYSTALS OF SIMILAR COLOR. FLUORITE CAN BE SCRATCHED BY A KITCHEN CARVING KNIFE.

Some rocks born in the same environment also end up being totally different, both chemically and in appearance. The same cooling lava that makes obsidian also makes basalt. Basalt is probably as tough a rock as one can find. It doesn't shatter like obsidian, it powders when struck by, say, an iron mallet. Oil well drillers hate basalt because, although it can be drilled by a bit containing diamond, the drilling goes very slowly. Its crystals are so small you can't see them without a microscope. Yet an X ray or chemical test can determine almost immediately that basalt and obsidian are very different kinds of rock. Basalt is crystal-line, and its tiny, dense, tightly bonded crystals create an extremely durable rock.

The Properties of Crystals

Every crystal has certain properties that distinguish it from other crystals. To a gem cutter, a crystal's defining characteristics have to do with the way light reacts to the stone and with its hardness and density.

Hardness is measured by the ability of a hard substance to scratch a mineral. The Viennese miner-alogist Friedrich Mohs (1773–1839) devised a hardness test by choosing ten stones to which he arbitrarily assigned a hardness value. His test is relative—hard stones could scratch softer ones, but stones of equal hardness could not scratch each other. The test does not specify the degree of hardness difference between one level and another. Later, an absolute hardness test was devised by A. Rosiwal. The relative accuracy of the Mohs and Rosiwal tests is given in the table on page 48.

© Brian Parker/Tom Stack & Associates

© Gary Milburn/Tom Stack & Associates

AS INORGANIC
AS THIS APATITE
CRYSTAL MAY
APPEAR, IT IS IN
FACT COMPOSED
OF THE SAME
MATERIAL AS
OUR TEETH. THE
DIFFERENCE
BETWEEN THE
CRYSTAL AND A
TOOTH IS THAT THE
TOOTH IS BUILT UP
OF MANY TINY
GRAINS OF APATITE
WHEREAS THE
STONE IS A SINGLE
LARGE CRYSTAL.
APATITE, LIKE
FLUORITE, CAN BE
SCRATCHED WITH
HARD METAL—AN
IMPORTANT FACT
USED IN THE DESIGN
OF DENTIST'S
IMPLEMENTS
AROUND THE
WORLD.

Mohs Hardness	Mineral	Comparative Hardness	Rosiwal Hardness
1	Talc	Scratched by fingernail	0.03
2	Gypsum	Scratched by fingernail	1.25
3	Calcite	Scratched by copper coin	4.5
4	Fluorite	Scratched by iron knife	5.0
5	Apatite	Scratched by steel knife	6.5
6	Orthoclase	Scratched by steel file	37.0
7	Quartz	Scratches window glass	120.0
8	Topaz	Scratches quartz	175.0
9	Corundum	Scratches topaz	1,000.0
10	Diamond	Scratches everything	140,000.0

© Gary Milburn/Tom Stack & Associates

© Breck P. Kent

MOST OF US THINK OF TOPAZ AS A BRILLIANT SHERRY-COLORED STONE. BUT TOPAZ ALSO COMES IN VARIOUS PINKS, YELLOW, BLUE-GREEN, BLUE, RED, AND CLEAR. GEM TOPAZ CRYSTALS, SUCH AS THESE EMBEDDED IN CLEVELANDITE, CUT AND POLISH BEAUTIFULLY.

Cleavage refers to the fact that most crystals—even the superhard diamond—have weak fracture lines along which they can be broken easily. Cleavage is particularly important to gem cutters. By identifying the cleavage of a stone, a cutter can divide crystals into pieces that can be shaped into fine, perfect jewels. (The great Cullinan diamond weighed 3,106 carats when it was found, but in 1908 it was cleaved into three pieces. Even after that, the three pieces were the largest stones ever cut!) Today the worrisome labors of stone cleavers have been eased by diamond saws, which make the best use of the gemstones and almost eliminate the possibility of a cleavage gone awry.

The bonding electrons in a crystal atom's outermost shell are more cohesive in one direction than in another. Crystals may cleave very perfectly (euclase is an example), perfectly (topaz), and imperfectly (garnet). Some crystals, such as quartz, won't cleave at all; quartz fractures into lenslike chips.

© Bill Disney

AT 7 ON THE MOHS SCALE, QUARTZ IS HARD ENOUGH TO SCRATCH WINDOW GLASS. THIS PIECE HAS A LIGHT COATING OF MANGANESE DIOXIDE ON IT, WHICH GIVES IT A WHITE, METALLIC LUSTER.

Specific gravity refers to the density of a crystal compared with water. The specific gravity of nearly all crystals varies between one and seven. A value of seven means the stone weighs seven times as much as an equivalent volume of water. The hardest stones, such as ruby, sapphire, and diamond, are not always the densest; in fact, common glass is heavier than all three. These stones are hard because of the strength of their atomic bonds, not because of the number of atoms squeezed into a specific volume.

Color is the most important characteristic of crystals. A clear (colorless) crystal transmits light entering it without altering the light's color. If a crystal absorbs all the light (as with obsidian), the crystal appears black. If the crystal absorbs all wavelengths in the same proportions, the crystal appears milky or gray. If only certain wavelengths are absorbed, say blue or red, the crystal will take on the color blend of all the remaining spectral hues. Hence, if all colors but green are filtered out, the observer sees the crystal as green.

Relatively few elements affect the color of crystals. Those that do include iron, cobalt, chromium, copper, manganese, nickel, and vanadium, along with rarer elements such as uranium. Since the distance a light ray must travel through a crystal affects the amount of light absorbed, gem cutters cut lighter colored stones so that their light paths are longer and therefore the color is deeper. Conversely, a dark-hued stone is cut thinner—and even hollowed out on the underside if truly opaque, as in the case of certain garnets.

Certain crystals change color under artificial light—whether incandescent or fluorescent. Alexandrite is the most dramatic crystal of this type, changing from green in sunlight to red in artificial light. This effect occurs because artificial light is stronger in certain wavelengths than daylight.

Refraction happens when light enters a substance at one angle and leaves it at another. The most common example is a stick dipped in water. As it slides beneath the surface there is a noticeable change in the angle at which it seems to enter the water and what it looks like below the surface. This is a very simple way of explaining why diamonds and other gemstones are so brilliant to the eye. By judiciously combining facets that refract light and inner surfaces that reflect it, fine crystals can glitter with an astonishing array of colors and flashes. This quality is called fire and is one of the most valued characteristics of gems. Most crystals have an inherent ability to refract light entering them along two parallel paths, so that an image refracted through the stone appears doubled.

Luster is a quality that is hard to define but readily evident in crystals that have it. It describes the way a stone reflects light back to the eye and is directly related to the index of a crystal's refraction but not to the color of the crystal. Diamond is a good example: Its refractive index yields a very high luster as light

OPAL IS A BEAUTIFUL, FIERY GEM PRIZED FOR THE FLASH OF IRIDESCENCE THAT PLAYS ACROSS ITS SURFACE. IT WAS KNOWN DURING ANCIENT GREEK AND ROMAN TIMES, BUT BECAME POPULAR DURING QUEEN VICTORIA'S REIGN. THE QUEEN WORE OPALS FROM THE THEN NEW BRITISH MINES IN AUSTRALIA TO CREATE A POPULAR DEMAND FOR THE STONE. THE CANNY SCHEME WORKED, AND OPAL JEWELRY HAS BEEN POPULAR EVER SINCE. IN ITS NATURAL STATE (opposite page) OPAL GIVES FEW HINTS OF THE TREASURE WITHIN.

reflects and rebounds through its interior, and the very high polish of its surfaces yields the reflective equivalent of interior luster, *brilliance*. The luster of stones like opal and pearl are called fatty, metallic, pearly, silky, or waxy.

Asterism describes the starlike effect of sapphire and ruby. Asterism is due to the arrangement of variable bands within a crystal. When these are parallel and the stone is cut so its base is parallel to them an effect called *chatoyancy* is produced. Chrysoberyl is the stone most associated with the chatoyant, or cat's eye, effect. At other times the reflecting bands lie in four-, six-, and sometimes twelve-rayed stars. Master gem cutters know how to cut these stones into the characteristic dome shapes of star sapphires and rubies.

Opalization describes the change in a gem's color as it is rotated under the eye. Opalization occurs when spheres of cristobalite embedded in the silica of a crystal interfere with the reflection of light waves.

How To Make Your Own Crystals

You can easily discover the basic properties of crystals by making a few yourself. Dissolve some salt in a glass of cold water. Add more salt until some of the salt remains undissolved even after stirring and waiting. Pour the clear solution into another glass, being careful not to disturb the undissolved crystals at the bottom of the glass. Tie a thread to a stick or toothpick and lay the stick across the top of the glass with the string in the water. Put the glass where it won't be disturbed. After about a month small, cube-shaped crystals of salt will have grown on the string. The crystals will grow until all of the salt in the solution has been used.

© Aldo Tutino/Art Resource

© Brian Parker/Tom Stack & Associates

3

Science and Industry

THE BLUE TINGES
ON THIS QUARTZ
CRYSTAL COME
FROM AJOITE, A
COPPER-BASED
MINERAL. EARLY
MINERS OFTEN
LOCATED MINERALS
BY LOOKING FOR
CERTAIN COLORED
CRYSTALS. FOR
EXAMPLE, BLUE
AND GREEN CRYS-
TALS HAVE LONG
LED PROSPECTORS
TO COPPER.

Crystals, and the minerals of which they are composed, have been of such enormous use to us that we can accurately say they have helped make civilization as we know it.

Long before recorded history, people knew that crystal formations were signposts to useful mineral deposits. Certain kinds of crystals could make superior arrowheads, and others could be used for medicines. The great ages of human progress reflect an advancing knowledge of crystals and the minerals they contain, for example, the obsidian and flint of the Stone Age, the tin and mercury of the Bronze Age, the iron-rich minerals of the Iron Age, the mix of limestone and clay of the Concrete Age, the yellow-green uranium-rich autinite of the Atomic Age, and now the silicon of the Computer Age.

Crystals play an important role in today's household. The scouring powder we use to clean sinks and bathtubs consists of tiny fragments of powdered crystals—feldspar in the case of the best brands, manufactured abrasive crystals in many others. Portable radios and television sets, computers, hearing aids, telephone systems, automobile ignitions, spark plugs—all these began as bits of crystal that have undergone a complex manufacturing process.

The power of crystals extends far beyond the household. Crystals in the ceramic insulators on electrical poles protect our homes and offices from the electrical power they carry. Crystal ruby lasers and silicon computer chips form the heart of devices that keep track of our credit records, supervise our communications networks, direct rail and airline traffic, diagnose diseases, and turn radio waves into the sounds we receive as music and news. Our world would simply not exist without them.

The properties of the crystals used in these technologies are surprisingly few. Crystals refract light and often change its color, and this fact has led to their use in optical devices and jewelry. Some crystals are very hard, hence their use in cutting and grinding tools. Other crystals—notably quartz—vibrate when struck with electrical energy; these can be fashioned into devices that transform electrical oscillations into specific frequencies used in radio, radar, and television. Finally, some crystals only partially transmit electricity. These semiconductors are the heart of all our computers.

© Bill Kaunitz/Courtesy of African Gems & Minerals

Mining Crystals

To humans in early recorded history, the most important property of crystals was their association with deposits of valuable ores. The Egyptians and Sumerians smelted gold and silver and made copper alloys before 4000 B.C. By the time of the Bronze Age (roughly 3000 to 1000 B.C.) people knew that valuable metals such as gold, silver, copper, lead, and tin could be found near crystal deposits. By 2500 B.C. Egyptian ships imported gold from southern Africa.

To pull these valuable ores from the earth, early civilizations devised a simple mining technique that is used today. *Surface mining* began when nomadic travelers discovered exposed beds of crystals. They later discovered these crystal beds occurred near deposits of metal ores. The bright glitter of rose quartz and other crystals revealed the presence of gold and silver ore. Carried in baskets or leather pouches by

OCCASIONALLY, MINERS STILL FIND DEPOSITS OF PURE METAL. THE EARLIEST METALS WERE PROBABLY PURIFIED FROM "NATIVE" ORES LIKE THIS COPPER. THE TERM "NATIVE" DENOTES A METAL THAT NEEDS LITTLE REFINEMENT.

© Brian Parker/Tom Stack & Associates

workers or animals to central collection points, the raw ore was then either taken away or smelted on the spot. The crude process of separating metal involved breaking the collected rock into small pieces, then separating out the ore by water sluice or by sifting the rock through basketwork screens. This process was, by today's standards, hopelessly inefficient, but it produced enough refined ore to be smelted. These ancient miners had learned from potters how to build bellows-driven furnaces that could heat copper, gold, tin, and other ores sufficiently so that they would melt and could be collected in ingots at the bottom.

Early miners also developed *streambed mining*. Stones containing minerals washed downstream from their original seams, where the water broke them into pieces ranging from pebble-size to sand. To retrieve ore-bearing sands, workers plunged bamboo or other tubes into the sand, then lifted it out and poured it into baskets. Other workers used shallow woven pans with wooden spades attached to one end; they pushed the spade tip into the gravel, then tilted it back to wash the sand into the pan and separate the ore for processing and smelting.

THE MODERN
METHOD OF MINING
CLEAR QUARTZ
CRYSTALS.

© Bill Kaunitz/Courtesy of Gary Fleck

A much more dangerous method of mining was devised to reach mineral deposits deep beneath the earth's surface. In *deep-rock mining* workers wore olive-oil or nut-oil lamps, sweating profusely as they hacked out chunks of ore. The ore was taken to the surface in buckets—sometimes over slippery rope ladders—where it was processed and smelted. The first scientific mining geologist, Agricola (see page 26), depicted the labors of these miners in 1530, in a series of woodcuts in his pioneering work, *De Re Metallica*.

The Development of Manmade Crystals

Long ago the makers of mechanical watches learned that no matter how carefully they made their wheels and pinions, these parts still developed tiny amounts of friction which eventually wore them out. As with any metal-against-metal friction, the works of watches needed to be protected by something smooth. How-

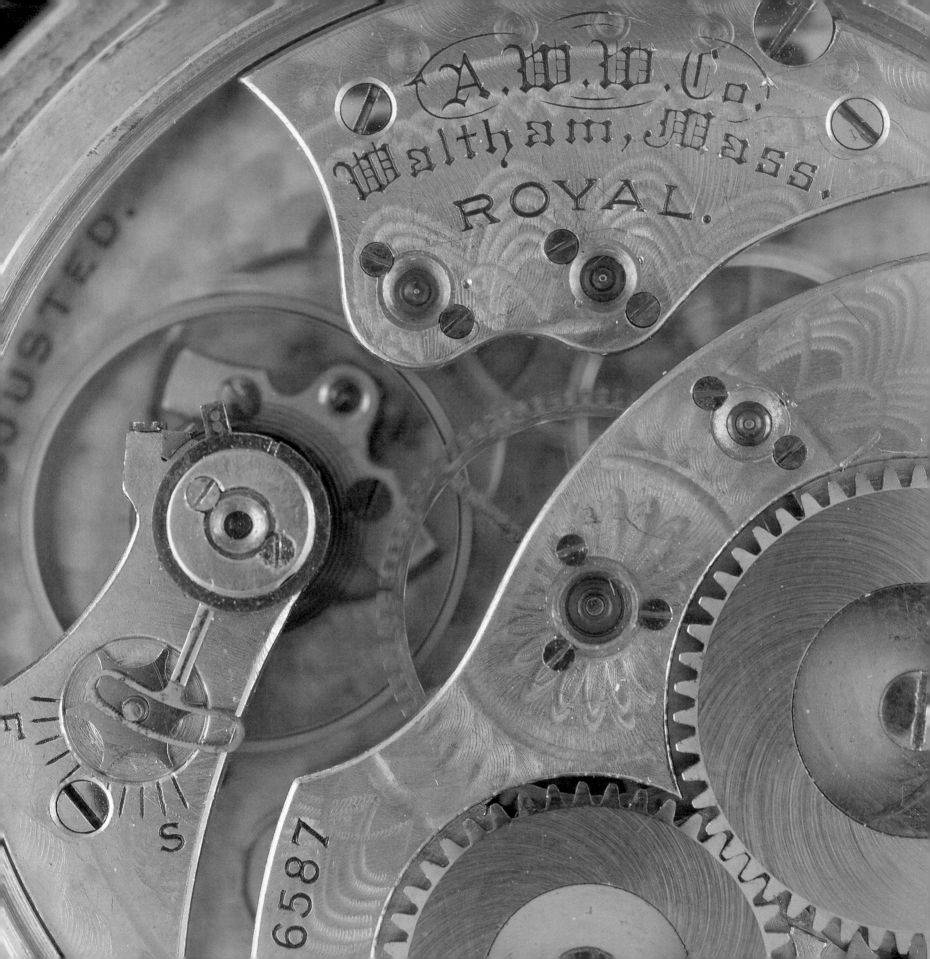

THE EARLIEST
INDUSTRIAL USE OF
RUBIES WAS AS
WATCH JEWELS.
RUBIES HAVE VERY
LOW FRICTION AND
ARE EXTREMELY
HARD (SECOND ONLY
TO DIAMONDS).
WHILE THESE
QUALITIES MAKE
THEM DESIRABLE AS
WATCH BEARINGS,
THEY ALSO MAKE
THEM VERY HARD
TO WORK, PARTICU-
LARLY IN THE TINY
SIZE REQUIRED IN
WATCHES, SO WATCH
DESIGNERS USE
THEM SPARINGLY.
ONLY THE VERY
HIGHEST QUALITY
WATCHES WOULD
HAVE HAD AS MANY
AS SHOWN HERE.

ever, even the finest watch oil is a petroleum product that will oxidize and become gummy with time, making the watch less and less accurate, and entailing an expensive cleaning job.

Jewelers, who usually sell both timepieces and gemstones, noticed that rubies were remarkably slippery to the touch, and next to the diamond— the hardest stone known—certainly harder than the metals used in watchmaking. During the 1840s a group of watchmakers in Geneva discovered they could use the bits and pieces of ruby left over from cutting natural stones into fine jewels as bearings for the escape movements in watches. They drilled V-shaped pits into the ruby pieces with almost microscopic chips of diamond, and voila!—watches with virtually no friction that didn't need oil. These jewel bearings were expensive. The number of them in a watch indicated the number of wheels in the watch's movement, which became an indication of the quality—and the cost—of a watch. That is the significance of labels such as *11 Jewels* or *21 Jewels* on the faces of many fine watches.

However, watchmakers soon exhausted the supply of ruby chips available from gem cutters, since rubies, carat for carat, are as valuable as diamond. Gemcutters naturally wanted to use every fragment they could as chips of color to accent larger stones.

Then, in the 1880s, gemlike rubies began to appear that, cut as jewels, looked natural. Upon close inspection with a jeweler's loupe, these "rubies" revealed an odd flaw—curious tadpole-shaped bubbles no larger than a speck of dust. Gemologists realized that these were no natural gems. The few bubbles that occur in natural rubies are almost always spherical, indicating that the hot liquid stone was motionless as it cooled. But tadpole-shaped bubbles indicated that the cooling liquid was moving. No one knew how it had been done, but these rubies were fakes.

While jewelers were thenceforth wary of anything that looked like a tadpole in a ruby, watchmakers took a different view. No one would see a bubble if it were inside a watch case. The demand for these ruby-like stones suitable for watches soon blossomed. Various laboratories in Europe raced to find ways to make "reconstructed" rubies.

Eventually a young Frenchman named Auguste Verneuil (1856–1913) developed a mass-production technique. Working in secrecy between 1886 and 1891, Verneuil developed a "flame fusion" process in which a fine powder of the ruby's basic building block, alumina, dropped through a tube into the extremely hot flame of an oxygen-hydrogen torch, where the powder melted into fine droplets that fell onto a ceramic rod. The cool rod caused the droplets to solidify on the rod.

THE SYNTHETIC QUARTZ USED TO MAKE RADIO OSCILLATORS MUST BE GROUND TO VERY PRECISE THICKNESSES. THE FINAL GRINDING, BEFORE POLISHING, IS DONE BY HAND. AFTER A FEW STROKES OF THE ABRASIVE DISK, THE CRYSTALS ARE MEASURED WITH A MICROMETER. WHEN THE PROPER THICKNESS IS REACHED, THE CRYSTAL WILL VIBRATE AT A VERY PRECISE FREQUENCY WHEN AN ELECTRICAL CHARGE IS APPLIED TO IT. THIS FREQUENCY IS THEN MODULATED ELECTRONICALLY TO PRODUCE THE MANY DIFFERENT TONES OF VOICE AND MUSIC HEARD ON THE RADIO.

© John L. Mutrex/Mutrex & Associates

By 1891 Verneuil began marketing his stones. By 1907 his production was over *5 million* carats (2,203 pounds or 990 kg!), resulting in an ample supply of watch bearings, plus plenty left over for use as abrasives and pigments. Today, more than a thousand factories use the Verneuil technique to produce tons of synthetic ruby, sapphire, and spinel (all variants of the same basic corundum crystal) each year.

Quartz, Radios, and Electronic Watches

Most of us think of the word *quartz* when we think of crystals in watches. *Quartz* signifies the presence of a tiny, meticulously prepared chip of quartz inside the watch. Why quartz? Why not topaz or pearl or opal?

Cheap, abundant quartz has a valuable property that rivals the gemstone qualities of its more exotic cousins, the diamond and ruby. When experimenters in the early part of this century subjected all manner of natural substances to various tests to discover how these substances were composed, they noticed that quartz has the unusual ability to briefly emit an electric current when pressure is applied to it at certain angles. This current is too small for the unaided human to detect, but properly amplified the current is very reliable and very exact. This effect was named piezoelectricity after the Greek word meaning "to press."

Being too small to detect without instruments, piezoelectricity seemed at first to be an interesting but inconsequential physical effect. But scientists wondered if there could be more. Experimenters asked what would happen if electrical current instead of mechanical pressure was applied to a quartz crystal. The experiment produced one of the most important scientific discoveries of our time. When a current was fed into a quartz crystal the crystal began oscillating at a frequency that depended not on the intensity of the current, but on the thickness of the crystal.

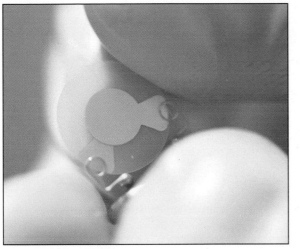

CRYSTAL FABRICATION IS NO EASY MATTER. ONE OF THE PROBLEMS IS THAT MANY CRYSTALS MUST BE VERY TINY IN ORDER TO BE USED. HERE A CRYSTAL BLANK IS BEING MOUNTED ON A BASE THAT WILL HOLD IT FIRMLY WHILE IT IS BEING GROUND AND SHAPED. THE "CEMENT" OFTEN USED TO HOLD CRYSTALS IS A REFINED PITCH WHICH ORIGINATES IN PINE TREES.

For a time quartz oscillation seemed a technology in search of a market. But as radio came out of the laboratory and changed from a scientific curiosity into a commercial product, quartz crystals suddenly became the cheapest and most reliable transmitters of radio frequency waves, and the cornerstone of the radio industry. (To this day the frequency of radio stations—with 50,000 watts or more of power—is controlled by a tiny quartz chip not much larger than a thumbnail.)

Then the drama of history intervened. In the late 1930s the best and largest quartz crystals came from Brazil—crystals so large that each could be sawed into thousands of radio oscillators. Manufacturers had become so dependent on Brazilian quartz that when World War II began, both Germans and Americans worried that the war effort might founder and the flow of sea traffic from the South Atlantic be cut off.

The Americans had plenty of serviceable native quartz (enough to make 55 million oscillator crystals, many used in walkie-talkies), but the Germans did not. They embarked on a crash program to make artifical quartz, using techniques developed in 1908 by the German physicist Richard Nacken (1882–1943). After the war American scientists discovered that Nacken's laboratory was well on the way to perfecting a technique that used high pressure and heat to form large artificial quartz crystals.

After this discovery, Bell Telephone Laboratories, Antioch College, and many other laboratories began experiments that resulted in commercial quartz manufacturing methods that, among other things, enabled watchmakers to put a tiny, precise chip of quartz inside watchcases and harness their power to tell time better than by any other method.

Crystals in the Computer Age

But the most inspiring story of our technical mastery over the powers of crystals is only now being played out—and in fact it may never end. It began even before the radio oscillator made of artificial quartz.

The electronic age as we know it goes back to 1907, when the American inventor Lee De Forest (1873–1961) made an improvement on the crude diode electron tubes that captured radio waves. De Forest added a third filament, which gave vacuum tubes the ability to amplify radio waves in addition to detecting them. This made radios possible, and soon a radio could be found in many homes across the country.

Vacuum tubes had several disadvantages. They were bulky, their glass covers broke easily, and they generated a lot of unwanted heat and wasted a lot of electrical power. As long as these problems were confined to radios that brought Bing Crosby and radio mysteries into homes, there was little need for improvement. With the development of computers, electronic equipment began to outgrow the bulky, hot vacuum tubes. The first electronic computer, built during World War II, required thousands of vacuum tubes. The defects of the vacuum tube magnified into uncontrollable problems.

In 1948 Bell Telephone Laboratories announced that they had managed to condense all the electrical properties of the vacuum tube onto a tiny semiconductor made of artificial silicon and germanium crystals. They called it a transistor because it combined the properties of an electrical *trans*mitter and an electrical re*sistor*.

Transistor semiconductors only partially conduct electricity. Their electrical flow can be regulated by varying the electrical voltage—the "pressure"— fed into them. By carefully sandwiching two or more different semiconductor materials, scientists found they could duplicate (and even dramatically improve) the performance of vacuum tubes—plus reduce the heat output to nearly zero and miniaturize them so that they were tinier than the petal of a buttercup.

From this tiny chip, a great technology has grown. It didn't take electrical engineers long to realize they could design silicon/germanium chips to contain nearly every electrical device known—resistors, diodes, rectifiers, and so on. These were called integrated circuits and form the heart of 99.99 percent of all the electronic devices manufactured today.

Integrated circuits make it possible to produce television sets that fit inside a cigarette package, wrist radios better than the comic strip detective Dick Tracy ever wore, telephone switching systems, portable and car telephones, hearing aids that fit almost invisibly into the ear, communications satellites, airline

© Tom Tracy/FPG International

SINCE NO ONE CAN SEE A LASER BEAM IF THE AIR IS CLEAR, TECHNICIANS DEMONSTRATE THE OPTICAL PATH TAKEN BY THE BEAM BY BLOWING A THIN SMOKE OR AEROSOL ACROSS THE PATH (AS SHOWN HERE). THE LASER BEAM REFLECTS OFF THE PARTICLES.

ticket reservation systems, airplane navigation systems that guide a plane to within 250 feet (76 m) of a runway after a five thousand-mile (8000 km) flight, the electronic ignition systems in today's automobiles, pocket calculators, and computers that handle billions of calculations in a second. Integrated circuits rest on the bottom of the sea floor, transmitting data to research vessels on the surface, and are now flying out past the sun aboard the only satellite humankind has ever launched into the heart of our galaxy.

Laser Technology

Although we are familiar with the lasers used at supermarket checkout counters and we hear about attempts to use them to produce fusion energy hotter than the interior of the sun, few people realize that many lasers employ crystals. Lasers work in much the same way as quartz oscillators. The various types of crystals used in lasers amplify electromagnetic radiation injected into them, then align it in such a way that

SINCE THE OPTICAL PATHS OF LASERS ARE EXTREMELY NARROW, EQUIPMENT MUST BE CALIBRATED VERY PRECISELY IF THE BEAM'S MEASUREMENTS ARE TO BE OF USE. LASER SYSTEM TECHNICIANS WEAR GOGGLES TO SHIELD THEIR EYES FROM THE BEAM. (Opposite page) THE FOCUSED BEAM OF A POWERFUL LASER CAN PRODUCE TEMPERATURES HOTTER THAN THE SURFACE OF THE SUN. EVEN THE HARDEST AND MOST TEMPERATURE-RESISTANT SUBSTANCES ARE NO MATCH FOR SUCH POWER. SINCE A LASER BEAM CAN BE FOCUSED TO WIDTHS FINER THAN A HUMAN HAIR, LASERS ARE OFTEN USED TO SHAPE MATERIALS THAT CAN'T BE CUT ANY OTHER WAY.

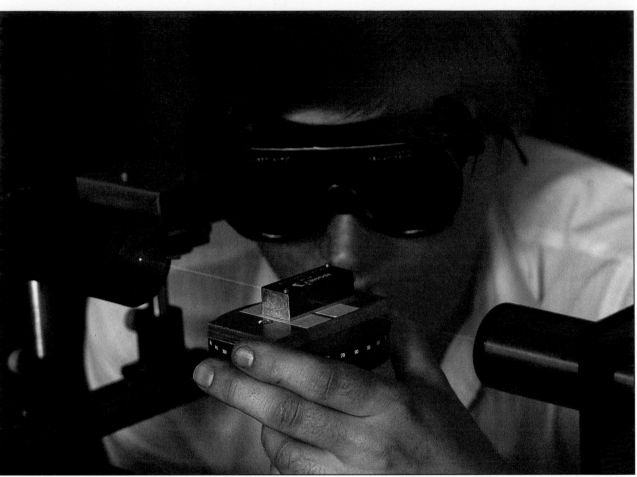

© Robert Rathe/FPG International

a beam of laser light travels in a nearly perfect parallel beam. Today lasers are used to align pipelines, buildings, tunnels, and other structures.

The Stanford Linear Accelerator in California was aligned to 1/50 (1/20 cm) inch over the length of a mile (1.6 km) using a laser beam. A laser in an airplane flying at 10,000 feet (3049 m) can detect the difference in height between a street and a sidewalk. Laser gyroscopes are ten times more accurate than the spinning wheel variety because they are immune to the forces of gravity and acceleration.

The ability to focus laser beams to extremely sharp points has enabled ophthalmologists to "weld" a detached retina to the inner surface of the eye, thus saving a patient's sight. Other physicians use lasers to remove tumors without damaging adjacent tissues and to cauterize tissues cut during surgery. Shipbuilders use much more powerful lasers to cut through the steel of a hull. Garment makers use lasers to cut cloth to tolerances as fine as a single thread. Focused lasers can drill holes in diamonds— and also burn clean holes into the nipples of baby bottles while leaving them completely sterile.

© G & M Kohler/FPG International

© Scott Camazine

THESE SALT CRYSTALS HAVE BEEN MAGNIFIED SEVERAL HUNDRED TIMES AND ILLUMINATED WITH COLORED LIGHT. A HOUSEHOLD MAGNIFYING GLASS ALONE CAN REVEAL SOME OF THE DETAILS SHOWN HERE—BUT A MICROSCOPE OF 100 X OR MORE CAN REVEAL AN ENTIRE WORLD OF NEW AND UNUSUAL CRYSTAL BEAUTY.

Lasers help predict earthquakes, measure pollution, and carry millions of phone calls along a single optical fiber hardly larger than the lead of a pencil. As scientists have improved the techniques of laser production by using crystals other than ruby (and even gases), they have devised lasers so efficient that some lasers can run over a million hours on the power supplied by a flashlight battery.

Crystals at Home and at Work

Crystals are equally important for our most mundane human needs. Wash basins, toilet bowls, and kitchen sinks are nothing more than crystalline substances that have been fused by heat into a dense porcelain mass—just as hard, beautiful marble has been fused from crumbly limestone.

Even the household scouring powder we use to clean these objects is an industrial crystal. In fact, the abrasives industry relies almost entirely on artificial crystals. Silicon carbide was first synthesized in 1891 from a mixture of sand, coke, sawdust, and salt heated to 2,400 degrees centigrade. Second only to diamond in hardness, this abrasive is the basis for the world's optical industry. Tiny lenses that fit on the ends of optical fibers that can be inserted into blood vessels are ground with the same crystalline abrasives that made the majestic Mount Palomar telescope in California, which peers out nearly to the edge of the universe.

Engineers soon realized that the same enormous heat required to melt silicon carbide made it an ideal material to line industrial furnaces and heat dissipators. Then they discovered silicon carbide has the unusual electrical property of becoming less resistant to electricity as the electrical voltage increases. This was an ideal property for a lightning rod, through which enormous bursts of electricity must be carried very quickly; other materials would simply vaporize. The thin wire you see sticking up from a church steeple, chimney, or tall building holds an artificial crystal quietly waiting to disarm a single thunderous blast of lightning energy that lasts only a thousandth of a second.

Even the salt on our tables has a fascinating story to tell about the industrial use of crystals. The sodium in salt's sodium chloride, as well as fluorine, bromine, and iodine, are elements that share the generic name halides. Pure salt and other halide crystals up to half a ton in weight are grown in ingots as large as a yard across. Salt and the other halides transmit infrared radiation very efficiently. A class of scientific instruments called spectrophotometers pass beams of infrared light through liquid samples in order to analyze the liquid's components very precisely.

Forensic scientists use spectrophotometers to analyze evidence taken at the scene of a crime. Quality control laboratories use them in food manufacturing plants to make sure the liquids in jars or cans indeed contain the ingredients on the label. Indeed, almost every commercial product depends on an infrared spectrophotometer at some point in its manufacture—gasoline, synthetic rubber, fibers such as nylon, beverages, and so on. And luckily for us, halide crystals are the easiest to shape into optical devices—they are cut to shape using a string dampened with water! If more laborious measures had to be employed, nearly every liquid product we use would cost a little more.

Scientists soon discovered other crystals that could be put to work. Today's technologists have found uses for sapphire that make this crystal just as necessary to our culture as salt. Sapphire (and ruby) are technically known as corundum. Sapphire possesses tremendous optical clarity and is extraordinarily tough. Next to diamond it is the hardest mineral, and it is five times tougher than glass. It is also chemically inert and has virtually no porosity, so substances can't adhere easily to its surface.

All these qualities add up to a very useful crystal. Industrial sapphire can be grown using the same Verneuil method used to make artificial rubies. In fact, commercial sapphire outshines natural star sapphires with its beautiful blue color.

However, for the best uses of sapphire, another process, called the Czochralski (Chuh-kral-skee) crystal-pulling technique is used. Instead of dropping alumina powder through a hot flame onto a rotating rod, the Czochralski method fills a crucible with molten alumina, then draws a crystal out of it by "freezing" it to a porcelain rod which is then slowly removed. The apparatus used looks like a high-tech drill press.

The colorless rods that emerge can be made large enough to cut into windows for helicopters and supersonic aircraft. Sapphire windows are so hard that bullets bounce off them and dust in the air moving past at 1,400 miles per hour (the speed of a bullet) won't streak them. Sapphire's toughness and resistance in hostile environments involving corrosive liquids or gases make it perfect for windows to observe and test chemical manufacturing processes that would frost or crack glass. Sapphire is also transparent to ultraviolet radiation (the opposite end of the visible spectrum from the infrared). It can therefore serve in the same kinds of spectrophotometers that use halide crystals. Spectrophotometers using sapphire test for phosphorescent effects that occur at much higher frequencies.

Sapphire is ideal for even the most mundane uses. It resists the damage that can be produced in many materials by laser beams, and is thus useful as a laser shield in military applications. Sapphire's hardness

RUBY AND SAPPHIRE ARE MEMBERS OF THE SAME FAMILY, CORUNDUM. THIS RUBY FROM TANZANIA IS EMBEDDED IN A WHITE STONE MATRIX OFTEN ASSOCIATED WITH RUBY AND SAPPHIRE. RUBIES AND SAPPHIRES HAVE SYMBOLIZED LUXURY AND GREAT WEALTH LONGER THAN ANY OTHER GEMSTONE—EVEN DIAMOND. LARGE RUBIES AND SAPPHIRES ARE INDEED MUCH SCARCER THAN DIAMONDS.

© Breck P. Kent

makes it valuable for the cutting edges of industrial milling machines, and for wear pads, washers, and bearings. A special continuous-pull manufacturing process can shape sapphire into pipes, rods, and beams. These are used to make instruments that cannot be made in any other way.

One would think that, given all this, the most precious crystal of all—diamond— would have as glamorous a series of uses as synthetic ruby and sapphire. Alas, that is far from the case. Diamond is made of carbon, as is the graphite in ordinary pencil lead. The difference between the two is the way carbon atoms bond at normal temperatures versus the way they bond at extreme temperatures and pressures deep in the earth.

On the surface of the earth carbon vaporizes at about 2,000 degrees centigrade. However, it does dissolve to a certain extent in molten iron and early attempts to make artificial diamond revolved around trying to crystallize it from a molten iron solution. The first attempts were reported over a century ago, in 1880 in Scotland. But only in 1955 was any success achieved. The General Electric Company announced that it had successfully made artificial diamonds by subjecting pure carbon to a heat of 5,000 degrees centigrade inside a special pressure-resistant chamber in a 1,000-ton press. These conditions approximate the heat and pressure deep inside the earth.

The General Electric process does not readily make gem-quality diamonds—the few such stones that have been produced are more expensive than the diamonds mined by traditional methods. However, the

© Breck P. Kent

THE CHARACTERISTIC "PIGEON'S BLOOD" COLOR OF RUBY IS CAUSED BY TRACE IMPURITIES OF CHROMIUM.

General Electric method makes superb industrial-grade diamond that comes in tiny black bits about the size of the period at the end of this sentence. These diamonds are produced in enormous quantities as abrasives and make it possible to drill inexpensive oil wells that supply the world with its major source of energy.

THOUGH THE BRILLIANCE AND CLARITY OF THIS FLASHY CRYSTAL RESEMBLE A DIAMOND, IN FACT, IT IS A "HERKIMER" —A FORM OF VERY CLEAR ROCK CRYSTAL FOUND ONLY IN HERKIMER COUNTY IN NEW YORK STATE.

Every one of the processes or products mentioned in this chapter figured in some way in the construction of the *Pioneer I* satellite sent to take photographs of the planets Jupiter, Saturn, Uranus, and Neptune. *Pioneer I* is now leaving the solar system, still sending signals to us on its way to the stars. We are now sending the fruits of our civilization to the very stars that provided the raw materials of our beginnings. Today, at the end of an investigative quest that produced all the mathematical and experimental evidence on which our scientific interpretation of the universe is founded, the journey is just beginning as we reunite our earth's atoms with the stars.

© Gary Milburn/Tom Stack & Associates

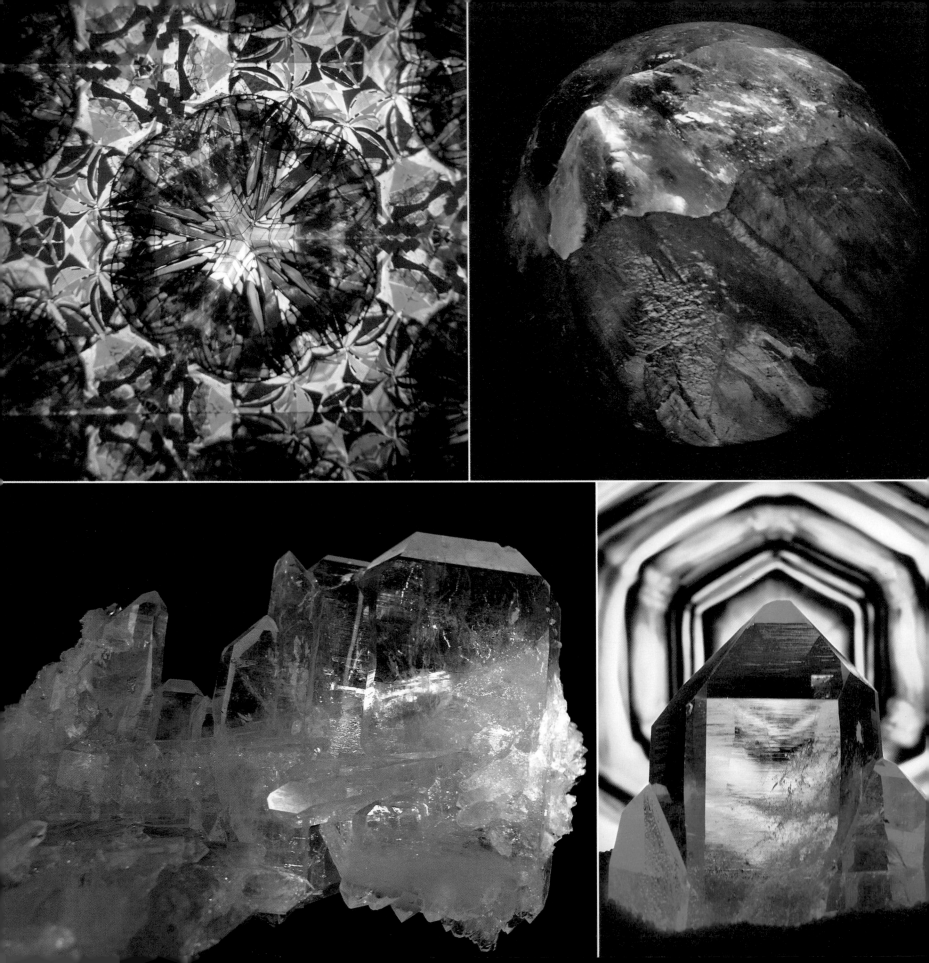

PART TWO

The Mysteries of

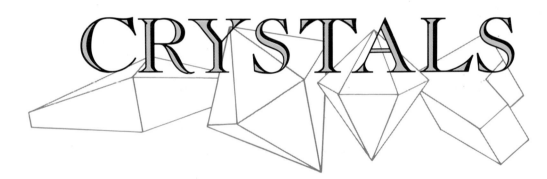

CRYSTALS

(clockwise from top left): © Bill Kaunitz & Dale K. Smith, © Bill Kaunitz/Courtesy of John Gibbon, © Bill Kaunitz/Courtesy of Gary Fleck, © Bill Disney

4

Crystal Energy

DOES THE APPELLATION "SMOKY QUARTZ WITH SKELETAL FACETING" TELL US ALL THERE IS TO KNOW ABOUT THIS CRYSTAL? IS IT ONLY AN AGGLOMERATION OF PHYSICAL ATOMS BOUND TOGETHER BY ATOMIC FORCES? IS IT ONLY SOME-THING BEAUTIFUL TO BEHOLD? IS IT ONLY A SMALL FRAGMENT IN AN INTRICATE ENERGY SYSTEM PERVADING ALL THINGS? ALL THESE THEORIES HAVE BEEN USED TO DESCRIBE CRYSTALS. ALL OF THEM ARE PARTLY TRUE, YET NONE COMPLETELY DESCRIBE THE CRYSTAL AND ITS PURPOSE ON EARTH.

Crystals play an important role in our daily lives. As we have seen, we use crystals every day—they are very practical objects. Yet crystals can affect our lives in other, more mysterious, ways as well.

Throughout history, peoples all over the globe noted that crystals possess healing powers and metaphysical energy. Words such as *shaman, talisman, healing, foretelling,* and *aura* continually appear in connection with crystals in the world's philosophical literature. In fact, crystals may well rank among the first objects humans considered to possess a power beyond their surface appearances. Today, with the emergence of *New Age* thinking, many believe crystals channel a spiritual energy that directly affects our lives.

While some dismiss New Age thinking with the argument that no hard evidence exists to prove that crystals have metaphysical powers, it is helpful to recall that even today some people dismiss scientific discoveries because they aren't mentioned in in the Bible.

Others believe that a fundamental constant links the material world of the scientist and the spiritual world of the metaphysician. That constant is energy. If, as physicists tell us, all matter is energy, then that energy passes through crystals, too. With their beauty and constant molecular structure, New Age thinkers believe crystals must possess some special powers to transmit that energy. Can there be a link between the physical and metaphysical worlds whose nature we can discover in the properties of energy?

Physical and Metaphysical Energy

Energy is the most intangible yet real phenomenon we experience. On the physical level we experience it directly when a weight pushes against us, infrared radiation warms our skin, or light of various colors strikes our eyes.

Other kinds of energy, however, reveal themselves much less directly. In the realm of physical energy, millions of tiny particles called neutrinos pass through us each second. We are totally unaware of them because they interact with other matter only exceedingly rarely. The earth's atmosphere is clothed in a vast

© Bill Disney

THIS CRYSTAL OF A LEAD MOLYBDATE HAS CONSIDERABLE ECONOMIC VALUE IN THE MOLYBDENUM IT YIELDS WHEN SMELTED, AND AESTHETIC VALUE IN ITS DELICATE HUES OF YELLOW MERGING WITH RED. BUT DOES THIS CRYSTAL HAVE A METAPHYSICAL VALUE AS WELL?

energy fabric of television and radio signals, but we become aware of their presence only when we turn on their receivers. Even more subtly, many physicists believe that solid matter—the electrons, neutrons, protons, and myriad subatomic particles—is a physical manifestation of energy transmission.

Metaphysical energy is even more mysterious. The impressive body of scientific literature we have built up since the time of the Greeks is paralleled by an even older body of literature that describes the effects of metaphysical energy—body auras, centers of body energy called chakras, the transmission of human energy from the past imparted by channeling, astrological energy that influences people's lives, and the all-pervading energy of a supreme being giving existence to all things.

No matter how we sense these various energies, we really detect only their effects. Scientists know that even their most advanced instruments measure only the results of energy, not the energy itself; they

© Gary Milburn/Tom Stack & Associates

describe energy's properties with mathematical formulas. Yet energy is a very complex and mysterious phenomenon. Often the ultimate source of a physical effect is many steps removed from the apparent cause.

An ocean wave crashing on a beach is an excellent example of the complex manifestations of energy. Oceanographers tell us that a wave results from energy imparted to the ocean surface by wind sweeping over a long expanse of water; this raises ripples that merge into waves whose growth depends on the force of the wind and the length of water over which it blows.

Yet the wind that creates the wave is far from the ultimate source of the wave's energy. A climatologist would say that the wind exists because of the uneven heating of the earth by the sun and the earth's rotation. An astrophysicist would add that the heat of the sun and turning of the earth ultimately come from the conversion of the universe's primordial hydrogen gas into radiation energy and complex elements. The cosmologist would point out that the primordial gas comes from a single immense big bang burst of energy 15 billion years ago, the effects of which we can deduce but whose cause eludes us. In short, the ultimate source of every phenomenon we know is a mystery. We simply do not know for certain how or why the universe came to be.

Most of us accept the fact that physical energy exists. But when it comes to metaphysical energy, many people are less certain. Some people readily accept that intangible philosophical phenomenon such as the one, the true, the good, and the beautiful exist and act on our perceptions in some way. Yet it is more difficult to grasp concepts like the transmigration of spirit energy, reincarnation, the nonphysical presence of ancestors in our lives, creating one's future lives, channeling, and the human energy body as part of God's energy body.

Perhaps the metaphysical ideas that New Age thinkers describe—auras, chakras, astrological influences, out-of-body experiences, crystal healing—are simply manifestations of a much larger energy transmission, just as the ocean wave ultimately originates with the creation of the universe.

Whatever the source of metaphysical energy or belief or nonbelief in it, many people do believe crystals transmit energy. Today crystals capture many imaginations (and have enjoyed a resurgence in fashion). An appreciation that crystals occupy a special place in our imagination is not a new idea. Understanding the role crystals have played in the history of adornment and metaphysics may put our modern fascination in perspective. Without crystal energy our earthly society might not have developed as it has.

Crystals in the Development of Civilization

Several lines of evidence reveal the tremendous impact crystals have had in shaping the course of history. These may also explain why we have attributed such "magical" powers to them.

On the practical level, crystals represented economic prosperity to early civilizations. Hunters first observed that many different kinds of animals instinctively found licks where certain cube-shaped crystals could be found. The hunters soon discovered these tiny crystals—salt—tasted good. Salt also attracted a steady stream of animals, some of which could be tamed. The droppings of all these animals passing through made the grass more plentiful near the salt licks than at distances farther away. Some peoples also found they could preserve meat with salt.

If people could take possession of salt licks and control them, they could use the salt for their own needs and use it for trade. Fixed possessions eventually became more important than moveable goods and

SALT IS PROBABLY
THE FIRST
CRYSTAL FOR
WHICH HUMANS
RECOGNIZED A
PRACTICAL USE.

© Breck P. Kent

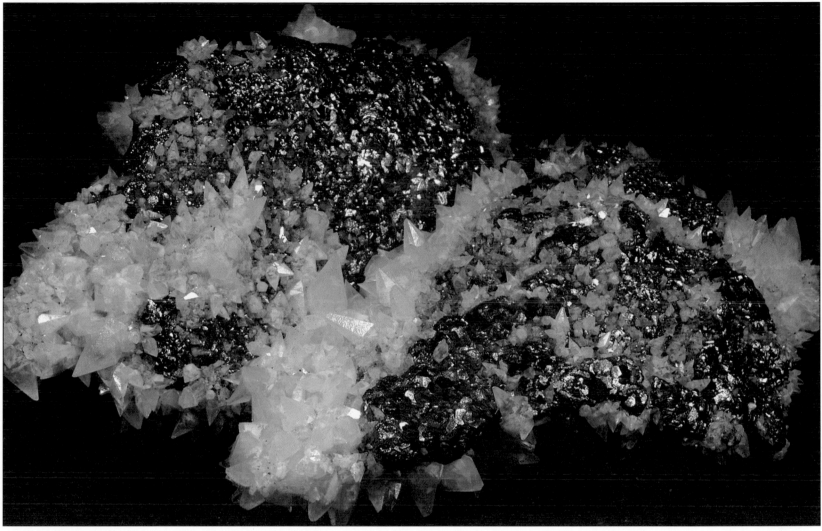

ALL THAT GLITTERS IS NOT GOLD. THIS IS PYRITE, AN IRON SULFIDE KNOWN AS "FOOL'S GOLD."

controlling other people through property could improve one's own living standards. Hence very early in human development crystals were related to two of humankind's most powerful motivators: food and power.

Historically, crystals were also said to possess healing powers. Though early peoples first may have noticed crystals for the way they attracted animals or glittered among other stones, it wasn't long before they began to investigate crystal properties for the way they affected the body. The fact that salt made food taste better must have triggered a good deal of experimentation with other substances from the earth. The first substances to try, of course, were the muds surrounding the salt lick—if one useful crystal was there, perhaps there were others as well. Over time (and probably after a lot of accidental deaths) people discovered certain other healing properties in the raw earth.

© John Cancalosi/Tom Stack & Associates

© Rick Cowley

THE STONES ON THIS PAGE AND THE DEPOSIT ON THE NEXT, ALTHOUGH VARIED IN APPEARANCE, ARE ALL MALACHITE. THE GREEN COMES FROM HYDRATED COPPER CARBONATE; OTHER COLORS COME FROM TRACE ELEMENTS.

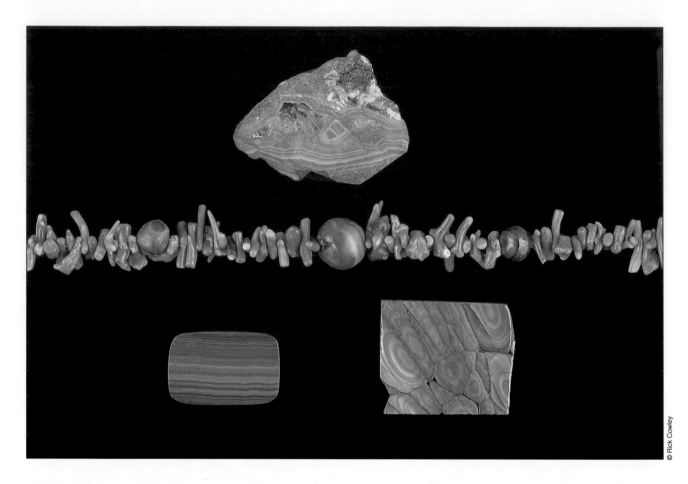

Alkali beds would have been one. Sooner or later people would have found that certain earths and the ashes from fires could calm an upset stomach. Today we know that alkali neutralizes stomach acidity. While today's alkali comes in the form of refined antacid tablets, early peoples simply ate alkaline earth or ashes. Other substances, such as borate crystals, could cleanse wounds, ease eye inflammations, and heal in other ways. Still others had the opposite effect: They were poisonous. Powdered beryl crystal, for example, is such a slow-acting poison that Renaissance assassins preferred it to faster products so the evidence would less likely point to them.

As healers experimented with various crystals and other substances, considerable lore developed around their magical properties. For example, the green of malachite resembles the green of nature, indicating an affinity with earth and water; therefore powdered malachite should be used to help a sickly child grow. Hematite, when crushed, has a reddish color nearly that of blood; therefore it cleans the body's blood and can protect warriors from harm. Many primitive warriors rubbed crushed hematite mixed with fat over their faces to make war paint.

© Rick Cowie™

Crystals also came to be used for artistic expression. The bright colors of powdered crystals could change an object's color. More than 20,000 years ago tribes in what is now central France and northeastern

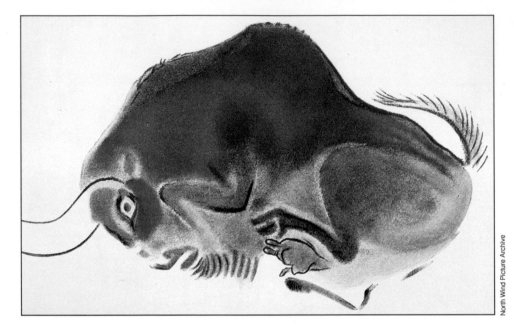

Spain crushed stones and mixed them with animal fats, vegetable oils, or water, creating colorful pastes that would retain their color after they dried. They painted vivid horses, bisons, goats, and hunters in caves that to this day dazzle the eye with color and artistic feeling. Lacking the brushes and spatulas of a modern painter's studio they used their fingers, palms, balled-up fists, elbows, forearms, even their hair.

Fire is perhaps one of the most fundamental crystal powers to be discovered by early humans.

THIS STONE-AGE CAVE PAINTING FOUND IN ALTAMIRA, SPAIN, WAS MADE WITH PIGMENTS FROM POWDERED CRYSTALS. IT IS OVER 20,000 YEARS OLD.

Crystals were probably first admired because of their gorgeous colors and their ability to reflect sunlight into brilliant bursts of light and refract it into rainbows of dazzling hues. To anyone, primitive or not, these are formidable properties. Yet the discovery that clear crystals, especially quartz, can crudely concentrate the sun's rays into a point so hot it can set dry leaves or grasses aflame must have been a remarkable feat. Other crystals, such as flint, could, when struck, make sparks that set tinder ablaze so that food could be cooked. Portable fire must have seemed like unbelievable magic to the person who first discovered it.

Crystals became useful for other needs as well. Some crystals broke into jagged edges that could be used to wound an animal, cut off its flesh, skin it, and scrape its bones. With such a variety of useful properties, it is no surprise that people began to think of crystals as some form of divine presence that gave them powers they could not otherwise achieve.

Another discovery about crystals contributed to the idea of their magical power, though in an indirect way. Eight thousand years ago, peoples in several different parts of the world noticed that cooking fires built on damp mud would bake the mud into a hard slab. This led to the invention of pottery. Though the first people to fire urns and figurines didn't realize it, making pottery involves a host of complex chemical changes that occur when a substance composed of many tiny pieces of crystal and other rock is heated to a high temperature. As water is removed and the substance dehydrates, oxygen and carbon are added. These two elements initiate other chemical reactions that result in the tiny particles fusing into a single hard object. One substance becomes another—due in large part to the properties of crystals.

As primitive peoples experimented with pottery, they noticed two things: Some pots had incompletely fired spots that would dissolve when the pot was placed in water. They also noticed that lighter colored streaks appeared in these soft spots. Perhaps this is how humans learned to glaze pottery. By painting the pots dark colors before they were fired, they would get hotter as the fire raged—after all, did not a person wearing a dark garment in front of a fire feel the heat more?

EARLY HUMANS USED CLEAR QUARTZ CRYSTALS LIKE THIS ONE TO START FIRES BY DIRECTING A BEAM OF SUNLIGHT ONTO GRASS.

© Bill Kaunitz/Courtesy of Brian Cook

DESPITE THEIR SURFACE APPEARANCES, METALS ARE COMPOSED OF CRYSTALLINE STRUCTURES. MOST METALLIC CRYSTAL GRAINS ARE SO TINY THEY CAN'T BE SEEN WITHOUT A MICROSCOPE. OCCASIONALLY METALS CRYSTALLIZE DURING FORMATION JUST AS NONMETALLIC MINERALS DO. THE CRYSTALS HERE ARE PURE GOLD. GOLD AND COPPER HAVE A GREATER PROPENSITY TO CRYSTALLIZE THAN OTHER METALS.

For glazes, these early potters crushed various crystals into powders, mixed them into the same kind of slurry they used to make other kinds of paints, then daubed it on the pots. However, the crystal colors they painted did not always end up the same color. Blues turned to browns, reds turned to green, and whites to gray. And, these changes could not always be predicted—a glaze that would turn red near the edge of the fire would turn black if the pot were in the middle. Without knowledge of the chemical changes taking place it must have seemed that an invisible magical presence in the fire and air caused such things.

If fire and air possessed mysterious qualities that changed a substance from one thing to another, could not the same be said for other elements—earth, and water, for example? If these four elements embodied some invisible power, what was that power? And if an invisible power energized these changes in simple things like air, earth, water, and fire, what power gave energy to life? If a powdered crystal could heal, why couldn't it heal just by its presence? If a powdered crystal could change the color of a pot by being put into a fire, perhaps the crystal had a secret power whose source was somewhere else? If all these effects were simply the end result—like the wave on the shore—what or where was the cause?

Similarly, speculations like these must have crossed early humans' minds when they discovered they could purify and strengthen metal by controlling fire. Except for mercury, most metals are in fact composed of tiny crystals, though their crystalline structure often is invisible to the eye. But no matter how these metals appeared originally, once they were melted by fire they could be formed into just about any shape—early knife blades were cast by pouring molten metal into furrows traced by a finger in sand.

The metalsmith was first helped by the potter, who had learned that blowing air into a fire with a bellows would make it hotter and bake harder pots. The smiths improved that idea by enclosing the fire and creating what we now know as a forge. They then learned that by pounding red-hot metal it would become harder. They recognized the advantages of this but didn't know that forging reduces the size of the metal's crystals and makes them less likely to crack.

Smiths also learned that by combining two or more metals they could come up with a new metal whose properties were better than the original metals. Humankind entered the bronze age when someone discovered that tin mixed with copper could make a spear point harder than any other metal. Over time smiths discovered a host of other metallurgical tricks, such as forcing air through molten metal with a bellows, which we now know oxygenates metal and removes carbon. Harder metals successively replaced softer ones, until in our own time we have stainless steel, which is virtually indestructable.

PERHAPS CIVILIZATION'S STRONGEST MOTIVATION IS THE DESIRE TO SEEK WHAT LIES BEYOND APPEARANCES. (Opposite page) TOWERING CRYSTALS ARE BELIEVED TO CHANNEL THE SPIRITUAL ENERGY OF THE UNIVERSE THE SAME WAY HUMANS CHANNEL PHYSICAL ENERGY.

Is Crystal Energy Metaphysical?

The very practical examples discussed above underline the fact that we can easily forget that crystals are associated with some of the most fundamental needs of our civilization—tableware, metal pans and earthenware bowls used to serve and cook food, healing agents made from natural products, the decorative arts we use to embellish our china, the glasses we fill with water (glass is amorphous rather than geometric crystal), the electrical insulators that brought moveable heat to the electric kitchen range, bricks that make the sides of a house, and the sense of private possession that makes a house a home.

These practical and magical applications of crystals throughout history illustrate their power. Perhaps they are nothing more than examples of our quest to understand and utilize the natural elements around us. Crystals have occupied such a high place in the consciousness of so many different peoples for so many thousands of years that it is easy to see why we might attribute magical powers to them. It can be said that crystals transmit an energy to us that has helped produce civilization. Perhaps the purely practical needs of humankind have some link with our spiritual needs.

© Bill Kaunitz/Courtesy of Gary Fleck

© Bill Kaunitz

5

Shamans, Healing Crystals, and Talismans

BLUE-WHITE TRANSLUCENT FELDSPAR, KNOWN AS MOONSTONE, SHIMMERS WHEN THE STONE IS TURNED. AS THE FELDSPAR CRYSTALLIZED IT FORMED INTO THIN LAYERS WHOSE "GRAIN" CRISSCROSSES LIKE A HERRINGBONE TWEED. THE EYE INTERPRETS THE INTERNAL REFLECTIONS AS SHIMMERING; THE EFFECT IS CALLED ADULARESCENCE.

Ancient and Modern Shamanism

The word *shaman* comes from the Russian Tungusic tribe's word for medicine man, *saman*, which in turn comes from the ancient Sanskrit word *sramana*, which means "healer monk."

Although the word shaman originated in these faraway lands, the idea that a medicine man or woman can cast out evil spirits and bring good can be found among peoples all over the world—Eskimos, Maoris from New Zealand, Mongolians, Polynesians, and Native Americans, just to name a few.

While many tribes have healers who know the basic facts of herbal lore, true shamans have had a transcendent psychological experience guiding them into a totally different state of consciousness. The world of the unconscious opens up, and the shaman falls into it. He or she comes to perceive that the ultimate importance of all things, including life, is to bring inner life into the outer world, teaching us to live in harmony with both the material and the spiritual worlds.

Though shamanism has become something of a fad, its roots reach back to earth's earliest cultures. In this era of high-tech medical equipment, well-staffed hospitals, and highly trained physicians and nurses, shamans thrive even in our modern society—although they may not regard themselves (or be generally thought of) as such.

William James, in his *The Varieties of Religious Experience*, describes shamans as having undergone "vital spiritual experiences which appear to be in the nature of huge emotional rearrangements." Ideas, emotions, and attitudes which were once guiding forces of people's lives are suddenly cast aside and a completely new set of conceptions and motives begins to dominate them. Bill Wilson, the founder of Alcoholics Anonymous, experienced such a transformation, which he described as "a destruction of self-centeredness." He went on to found a program for healing that has affected the lives of millions suffering

© William Cornelia

from the disease of addiction. Wilson is an example of the shaman in our own time, a spiritual explorer who performs healing tasks related to the body's disharmony with the soul.

The word *healing* has appeared continually throughout this book, but what, exactly, does it mean?

Nearly everyone experiences life as a process of growth—physical maturation on one hand and growth in our levels of consciousness on the other. When we are ready to enter into a new state of consciousness, we often experience disease. Taken as "dis-ease"—being out of harmony with one's soul— the word *disease* can mean many things: common physical ailments, addictions and addictive behavior, denial, lack of love for the self and others, spiritual malaise, misuse of power, or will to evil. In all these cases, the physical or spiritual disease is one thing, its cause is another.

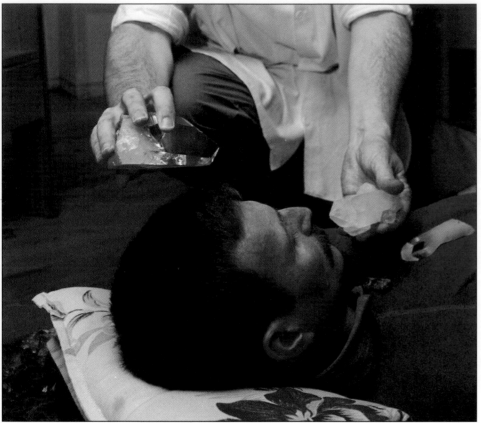

© John Raineri

To heal, whether physically or spiritually, it is necessary to learn the cause of the "dis-ease" and to realign one's personal energy with the energy that pervades the universe.

Shamans can help do this, but shamans—as one might expect from the preceding description of their powers—are not to be found on every street corner.

CRYSTALS HAVE BEEN EMPLOYED AS HEALING AGENTS SINCE BEFORE RECORDED HISTORY. CERTAIN CRYSTALS ARE BELIEVED TO AFFECT CERTAIN PARTS OF THE BODY. EMERALD, FOR EXAMPLE, IS SAID TO HEAL AN AILING LIVER.

New Age thinkers believe that we can *self*-heal. Crystals have become a popular tool in this healing process, because they help to balance the body's natural healing system.

Body Energy: The Chakras

According to many who use crystals, the physical body is more than skin, muscle, and bones. It is a form of energy, just as the atoms and stars are energy forms. Take energy away, whether in the form of food, water, air, or spirituality, and the body breaks down. The total human is a series of energy systems connecting the mind, the body, the emotions, and the life force or soul.

The crystal possesses energies that can resonate within the individual and help people become sensitive to their own energies. This awareness can then be worked with to realign personal energy with universal energy. Crystals, it is said, have the power to harmonize energy systems and create changes that will manifest themselves in the physical body. Crystal healing doesn't deal with the physical body in the way that herbal or pharmaceutical healing does—a crystal won't cure the flu (and one should follow the medical program of a physician in dealing with the symptoms of a disease). Rather, crystal healing acts on the energy systems that create or destroy the spiritual system of the body.

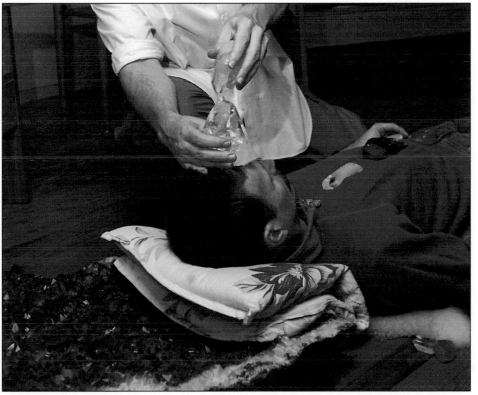

THE PURPLE RAY OF AMETHYST IS BELIEVED TO OPEN THE THIRD-EYE CHAKRA IN THE FOREHEAD TO ALLOW WISDOM ENERGY TO FLOW FROM THE HEAD.

© John Raineri

The body—like the earth and the universe—is a complex set of energy waves. The brain, for example, has four detectable waves. Alpha waves range from seven to fourteen cycles per second and are most prominent while one is dreaming. Beta waves average about twenty-one cycles per second and are strongest when we are fully conscious and going about our daily tasks. Theta waves range from four to seven cycles per second and are associated with deep trance states and extrasensory perception.

Delta waves range from one-half to four cycles a second and occur when we are in deep sleep.

Thus the mind, too, is an energy form and, like other energy forms, can be modulated. Hypnosis and meditation are two well-known methods of such modulation. Some people think that symbols, myths, and archetypes, rather than the conscious mind's linear flow of words, are the language of the subconscious mind. Crystals can channel the flow of the unconscious mind's imagistic energy to produce powerful creative and dreaming capabilities.

The body also has its energy centers. You can feel some of them quite readily—the centers of the palms, insides of the elbows, the "third eye" slightly above eye level at the center of the forehead. Others are more subtle. Ancient clairvoyants saw seven such energy centers, which resembled spinning wheels of light; these clairvoyants called the energy centers *chakras*, which in their language, Sanskrit, means "wheel."

The first, and lowest, of the seven chakras is the root, which is located in the genital area and covers them. The second is between the genitals and the stomach, about two inches (5 cm) below the navel; it stimulates the internal reproductive system. The third is the solar plexus, slightly above the navel; it affects the stomach. The heart, or fourth, chakra is in the center of the chest; it is said to stimulate the thymus gland. The fifth chakra is centered in the throat and works with the thyroid gland. The sixth chakra is at the brow and corresponds to the ancients' "third eye," located in the middle of the forehead about half an inch (1.3 cm) above the eyes; it controls the pituitary gland. At the crown, or very top of the head, the seventh chakra works in conjunction with the pineal gland.

The chakras are said to deal with the movement of life energy throughout the body. The body channels energy via the chakras in the same way crystals refract and reflect energy by way of their facets. When the body is free from tension and fear, life energy flows unimpeded throughout, moved by the chakras to the various glands and organs they govern. But if a "dis-ease" of any of the kinds noted above affects the mind, the mind's brain waves obstruct and twist the healthy flow of energy throughout the body. The natural flow of energy from the mind through the rest of the body is altered, much in the same way that a dam in a small stream alters its flow. Energy fails to reach the chakras and hence the vital organs. Starved by a weakened and "dis-eased" life force, these organs become susceptible to the physical symptoms of disease. Modern medicine can do wonders to ameliorate the symptoms of disease, but as long as the root cause—an unbalanced flow of life energy— remains unchanged, the disease is never cured but only suppressed, masked, or made dormant.

Crystals and Healing

Beyond the chakras, crystals work subtly on other parts of the body's energy field. Many believe that the body's presence does not end at the skin's surface, just as the visible surface of the sun is not the end of its presence. The sun's surface appears to terminate at the photosphere, but a corona stretches above the photosphere for more than a million miles.

Scientists confirm that human bodies are surrounded by an electromagnetic field. We become aware of this field ourselves as we walk around a room while the radio or television is on. As we move around the room we can hear or see differences in transmission intensity and clarity. Stand in one part of the room

THESE CRYSTALS HAVE BEEN PLACED OVER THE SECOND, THIRD, AND FOURTH CHAKRAS—REPRESENTING RESPECTIVELY, THE SPLEEN, STOMACH, AND HEART. PLACING CRYSTALS OVER SEVERAL CHAKRAS AT ONCE UNITES THEIR ENERGIES.

and the reception is clear; in another the reception may be fuzzy. We can hear the changes in reception as we walk about—clearly our energy is affecting the radio waves' energy. It is not hard to visualize, then, why a crystal's radiative power interacts with electrical and much more subtle spiritual fields that emanate from the body. Crystals affect the body by influencing the etheric spiritual presence that extends beyond the skin. Crystals exert no forces in themselves—their energy fields merely channel other energies.

New Age thought maintains that crystals focus and harmonize energy and can clear imbalances in the chakra system. The point of the healing process is to harmonize self energy with the universe's energy. The term "New Age" means "The Age of Integration," and New Age adherents believe this age will heal divisions between the body and spirit and nature and humanity that have been forged through the ages. Crystal healers believe that integration can begin with the individual.

© John Raireri

© Bill Disney

LIGHT DARKENS WHEN PASSING THROUGH OR REFLECTING FROM A CRYSTAL AND BECOMES COLOR. YELLOW HAS ALWAYS BEEN ASSOCIATED WITH BRIGHTNESS, BEING ONLY A SLIGHT MITIGATION OF PURE LIGHT. YELLOW TENDS TO BE INTENSE, WHILE BLUE, ON THE OTHER HAND, IS RECESSIVE, EMPTY, GLOOMY.

Various crystal healing practitioners differ occasionally in their directives for the actual practice of crystal healing (the size of crystal to use, where to aim its point, whether or not to visualize one's disease while holding the crystal, etc.), but they are in agreement that the use of crystals helps people get in touch with some power.

Some people believe that crystal healing power is nothing but superstition, a placebo effect much like that of the sugar pills in place of an active drug in medical experiments. Sometimes this might actually be the case. Yet there is such an enormous body of lore and belief surrounding crystals' healing properties of crystals that there is a kernel of truth in at least some of them. With so many people promoting the power of crystal healing we can't completely discount the phenomenon as superstition. Nevertheless, there are unquestionably some foolish ideas being propagated which give credulous people the impression that crystals are a panacea for all of life's ills. (They will not, for example, magically change your life overnight or help buy you a new car.)

Crystals work not on the physical symptoms of a disease, but with the underlying spiritual "dis-ease," the disharmony between one's personal life energy and the energy pervading the universe.

Crystals, Talismans, and Healing Stones in History

A thirteenth-century book describes the properties of certain crystals thus:

> "A frog, engraved on beryl, will have the power to reconcile enemies and produce friendship where there was discord. A lion or an archer graven on jasper gives help against poison and cures fever. A bull engraved on chrysoprase gives aid against evil spells and to procure the favor of magistrates. The well-formed image of a lion, if engraved on garnet, will protect and preserve honors and health, and cures the wearer of all diseases and guards him from all perils of travel."

This passage shows that legends associating crystals with healing properties were already very advanced by the thirteenth century (when Chartres cathedral was built). It also illustrates that some believe the powers of a crystal can be enhanced if a talismanic symbol is engraved in it. Talismans are figures cut or engraved in an object, or an object considered to have extraordinary power in averting evil. A fourteenth century treatise counsels, "A good stone is one on which you shall find a graven or figured serpent with a raven on its tail. Whosoever wears this stone will enjoy high station and be much honored." An already powerful crystal can be made more powerful through a symbolic agent. And, unlike other healing agents such as herbs, crystal talismans do not have to be ingested into the body in order to have an effect; their mere presence wards off bodily or spiritual ills.

Today a large body of folklore exists about the healing powers of crystals on which talismans have been carved. For example, for thousands of years the Chinese have believed that jade carved with images of spirit figures would act as a purifying and cleansing agent; hence its common use as talisman intended to be placed next to the body, where the Chinese feel its influence helps free the body of toxins.

Far across the world, the Mayans used jade for the same purpose. In fact, jade's Western name comes from the antique Spanish term *piedra de yijada*, meaning "stone of the flank." The term derives from the Mayans' use of jade as a cure for kidney problems. Many anthropologists have noted the fact that uncarved jade is often used as an amulet by women in various cultures to ease the pains of giving birth. The written literature regarding jade as a cleansing stone even contains a quote by Sir Walter Raleigh:

> The Amazones have likewise great store of these plates of gold, which they recover by exchange, chiefly for a kind of green stone, which the Spaniards call Piedras Yijadas, and we use for spleene stones and for the disease of the stone we also esteeme them.

IF YELLOW AND BLUE—GAIETY AND MELANCHOLY—ARE MIXED, THE GREEN OF THIS EMERALD RESULTS. THE EARTH IS GRATEFUL FOR EMERALD BECAUSE IT BLENDS OPPOSING EMO- TIONS. HENCE THE EMERALD'S GREAT RARITY AND VALUE.

Hematite is another powerful healing stone. Long before chemists discovered that hematite is an iron oxide, various peoples associated hematite crystals with healthy blood. Iron, of course, is an element vitally needed in the manufacture of blood by bone marrow, and a deficiency of iron in the body produces a strength-sapping anemia. The relation of hematite to healthy blood has been noted as far back as the Greek physician, Galen (A.D. 129–ca 199), who prescribed it for inflamed eyes and headaches. The Roman savant Pliny the Elder (A.D. 23–79) also prescribed hematite as a cure for blood disorders.

© Breck P. Kent

Similar ideas about the powers of crystals pervade nearly every culture in the world. Ancient Druids used beryl crystals to foretell the future, and Scottish highlanders called beryl "the stone of power." Apache medicine men used crystals to induce visions and regain lost ponies. Australian aboriginals and the natives of New Guinea made quartz amulets to use in rainmaking ceremonies.

PLINY THE ELDER, THE FIRST TO CREATE AN ENCYCLOPEDIA OF NATURE, SAID OF THE SHAPING OF JEWELS, "THE PARTS OF A JEWEL INTENDED TO MAGNIFY COLOR MUST BE SMOOTH AND SIMPLE; THE PARTS INTENDED TO ENHANCE SHADE MUST BE MOTTLED AND TEXTURED. COLOR MUST BE REMOVED FROM ITS NATURAL STATE AND REMADE BY THE JEWEL."

© William Cornelia

Over time, people in many parts of the world came to think that crystals could also heal the soul's ills, just as willow bark, for example, could heal headaches (willow contains salicylic acid, the principle ingredient in aspirin). Bit by bit, through trial and error over thousands of years, an array of scattered information coalesced into a body of wisdom that slowly came to be shamanistic lore.

Pliny the Elder first wrote comprehensively about the shamanistic tradition in his enormous thirty-seven–volume encyclopedia *Historia Naturalis*. Pliny faithfully recorded ancient beliefs as well as the popular attitudes of his time. Red stones such as garnet, carnelian, and ruby were thought good for bleeding illnesses and rashes. Green stones cured eye diseases of the eye and blinded poisonous serpents if they looked upon the stone. The Hindu physician Teifashi stated in *A.D.* 1242 that emerald had the additional property of being able to cure intestinal complications such as dysentery. A sixteenth-century Spanish physician claimed that in order to cure dysentery one had to touch one emerald to the abdomen and place another emerald in the mouth.

There was a crystal or combination of crystals for nearly every ailment. Malachite was used as a local anesthetic and sapphire cured boils. Chrysoprase was considered a powerful fertility enhancer and a guard against sexually transmitted diseases.

Beryl (of which aquamarine and emerald are types) supposedly helps people avoid doing the unnecessary and is an aid to learning. It filters out distractions and unnecessary thoughts, and relieves stress and calms the mind. Gem healers also claim that beryl cleanses the circulation and lungs and makes them more resistant to toxins.

AQUAMARINES (below) ARE TRADITIONALLY LOVED BY LIVELY, INTENSE, ACTIVE PEOPLE. PURPLE IS THE COLOR OF CALM. AS HUMANKIND ENTERS THE AQUARIAN AGE, AMETHYST (opposite page) GUIDES OUR VOYAGE INTO PEACE.

The amethyst owes its name—and function—to the ancient Greek word meaning "not to be intoxicated." According to Greek legend, the god Bacchus was offended at some slight and decided he would take revenge on the first person he met by unleashing his guardians, a pair of tigers. Fate had it that this person was a beautiful maiden named Amethyst, who was on her way to worship at the shrine of Diana. As the tigers leaped toward Amethyst, Diana intervened by changing her into a pure, clear stone. Recognizing the intervention of Diana, Bacchus repented and poured his wine over the stone, giving it a violet hue that we have come to call amethyst. Hence amethyst came to be used to overcome drunkenness —and also to calm physical passion.

© B. Probstein/FPG International

© Bill Kaunitz/Courtesy of Chris Wight

© Bill Kaunitz & Dale K. Smith

THE CRYSTAL
KALEIDOSCOPE
IS A NEW AGE
METAPHOR FOR
OUR PERPETUAL
SEARCH FOR REIN-
CARNATION AND
ENLIGHTENMENT.

These writings are typical of those about crystals up until about the time of the Renaissance in Italy. They deal mainly with two subjects: detailed but uncritical descriptions of crystals' medicinal and magical powers and travelers' accounts of where various crystals could be found. Marbodus, the eleventh-century bishop of Rennes in France, emphasized the medicinal and magical properties of crystals in his *Lapidarium* (written about 1090). However, his work is filled with contradictions regarding the different virtues assigned to various crystals, and the qualities of a stone described in one part of his work are assigned to another stone somewhere else.

Marbodus established an unfortunate pattern that has continued up to today: the habit of copying without discrimination or personal critical appraisal whatever information has been written before. Some New Age thinkers still suffer from this shortcoming, hence the occasional statement that crystals are really parts of Atlantis that have floated to our shores. (The Atlantis myth will be treated in the next chapter.)

During the Renaissance and Enlightenment, the scientific interpretation of nature began to replace the spiritual explanation. Although early written treatises survived (in part because of the Renaissance reverence for Greek and Roman knowledge), a great deal of unwritten folk wisdom about crystals and many other natural healing agents was lost.

Today, thanks to the efforts of folklorists, historians of popular culture such as Keith Thomas, and cultural anthropologists such as Joseph Campbell—not to mention thousands of New Age practitioners all over the world—the importance of early mystical lore about crystals is being reappraised, and the power of crystals has become a legitimate study, or tool for personal growth, once again.

Crystal Talismans in Our Daily Lives

We practice some extraordinarily ancient customs without being aware of what we are doing. The engagement ring, for example, is one of the most common crystal talismans. Other talismans include bells, bracelets, earrings, necklaces, and seals. Practices as old as these testify to the fact that many people experience the spiritual effects of crystals.

What is it about crystals that make some people feel better in some undefined way simply by the act of wearing them? And why does jewelry—which is basically a talisman considered as an object of beauty—occupy such a high place in the world of fashion and personal adornment?

People throughout history have believed that every crystal has its own vibrational resonance, special influence, and function. Inherent within the nature of crystals is the ability to focus life energy. Life energy is a complex web of bodily and spiritual resonances governed by the mind. Crystals have energy levels of their own that can channel our life energy in ways that heal, energize, attune, and uplift the spirit of our inner beings.

GLASS IS THE CRYSTAL MADE BY HUMANKIND.

© Bill Kaunitz/Courtesy of Frank Cox

Quartz: The Earth's Healing Stone

Found all over the world, quartz is the earth's most abundant crystal and has long been valued for its beauty and healing properties.

Quartz is composed of silicon and oxygen, two of the most common elements on earth. In the form of silicon dioxide, these elements are also an important constituent of our bodies. The transfer of energy from quartz's silicon and oxygen to our body's silicon and oxygen may explain quartz's alleged healing properties. The ancient and highly esteemed therapeutic method of acupuncture acknowledges the effectiveness of quartz: People undergoing acupuncture treatments report that the treatment's effects are noticeably enhanced if the needles are coated with quartz crystal.

Quartz was perhaps the first crystal to be used as jewelry because of its seemingly endless supply and because it comes in many attractive colors—amethyst, blue quartz, citrine quartz, smoky quartz, rose quartz, and cat's-eye quartz. Though harder than steel, quartz is a fairly soft stone compared with topaz, sapphire, or diamond, and its cleavage lines make fashioning it into a variety of shapes, including crystal balls, relatively easy.

(Below) CITRINE QUARTZ'S COLOR IS CAUSED BY TINY AMOUNTS OF URANIUM. (Right) ROSE QUARTZ HAS ALWAYS BEEN CONSIDERED THE PRINCESS OF THE QUARTZ FAMILY. THE BEST SPECIMENS COME FROM BRAZIL.

© John Pearson/FPG International

© Bill Tronca/Tom Stack & Associates

Clearly quartz efficiently transmits energy. Much more scientific experimentation needs to be done on quartz's healing capabilities, but many people attest to its ability to regulate the energy flow of the spiritual body.

No two crystals are exactly alike, just as there are no two identical snowflakes (snow, of course, is crystallized water). Many people who study the metaphysics of crystals believe that a particular resonance of energies from the earth and the cosmos are captured within a crystal's atomic structure at the time of the crystal's formation. These energies, it is thought, give each crystal its particular spiritual qualities, just as the chemical impurities and radiation present at the crystal's birth imbue it with individual color and luster. A crystal's spiritual energy can be tapped as long as the wearer chooses to make use of the stone's spiritual presence. The belief that a crystal's spiritual energy comes from a power greater than itself implies that the power of a crystal does not wane with age or use; its energy comes from the universe.

Crystals, it is believed, work on the body and mind of the wearer regardless of whether these properties are understood by the wearer. However, a crystal's power can be enhanced if the wearer is conscious of its powers. With crystals, there is no such thing as a lucky or unlucky stone. In some areas of the world, magnetic fields around certain crystals make it possible for people attuned to the same fields to use the crystals for imposing their own will over others. Many people are attracted to certain crystals because of the vibrations that can be supplied only by that crystal. Upon seeing a particular stone, some people experience a sudden and impulsive desire to possess it. They don't know why, but they want to carry it in their pocket or wear it in the form of a ring or necklace.

© Scott Camazine

SNOWFLAKES GET THEIR DISTINCTIVE SIX-RAYED SHAPES FROM THE BONDING PATTERN OF WATER'S TWO HYDROGEN ATOMS AND ONE OXYGEN ATOM. IF NO TWO SNOWFLAKES ARE ALIKE, BEAUTY IS TRULY INFINITE.

Birthstones and Other Crystal Lore

The use of birthstones expresses the ancient belief that certain stones bring protection and luck. References to birthstones are found in the Bible in Revelations 21:18. Crystals have been linked to the effects of various planets and the twelve signs of the zodiac. The mystical use of the number twelve appears in ancient Jewish lore as the twelve tribes and in the twelve stones of the breastplate of the Jewish high priest. Early Jewish cabalists suggested that twelve stones, each engraved with an anagram of God, had mystical power over the twelve angels: ruby for Malchediel, topaz for Asmodel, carbuncle for Ambriel,

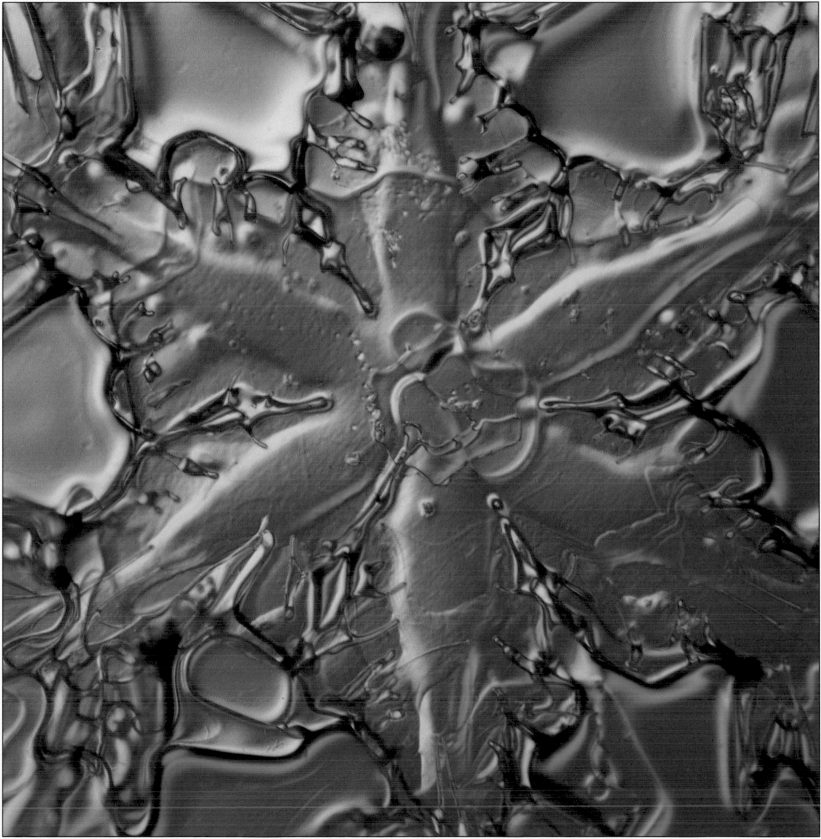

© Scott Camazine

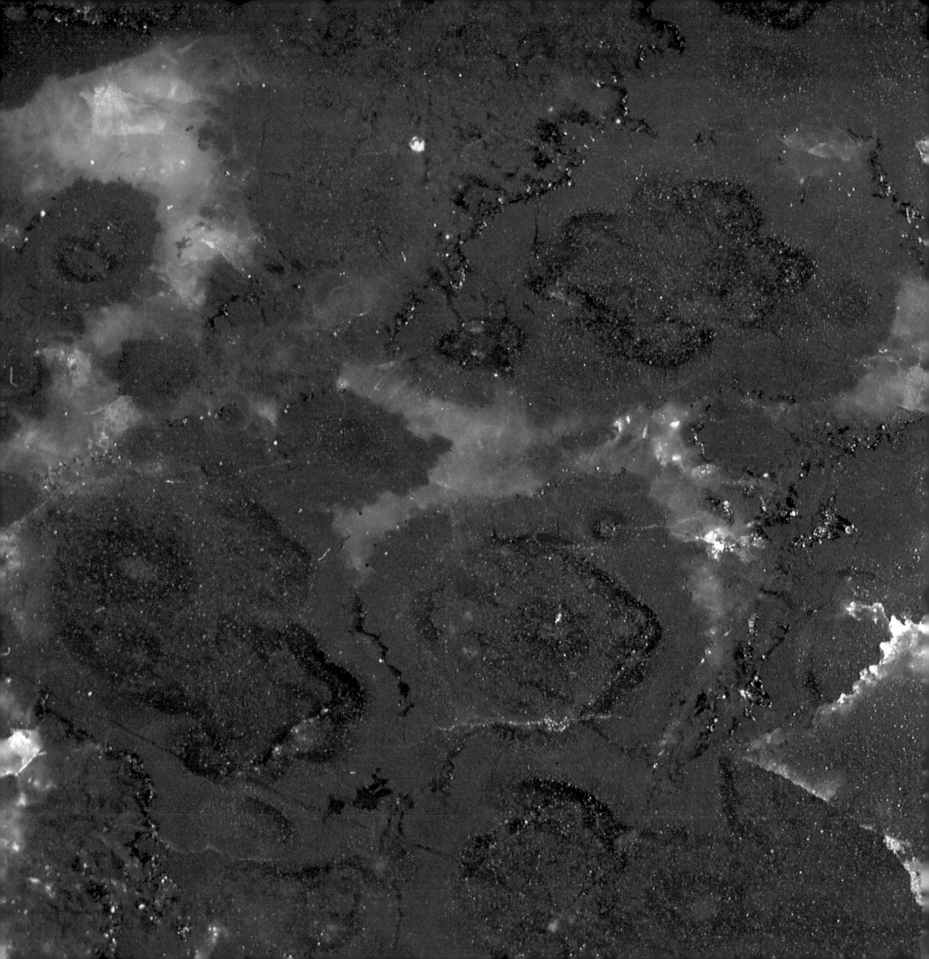

THE TWELVE APOSTOLIC STONES OF CHRISTENDOM

Apostle	Stone
Peter	Jasper
Andrew	Sapphire
James	Chalcedony
John	Emerald
Philip	Sardonyx
Bartholomew	Sard
Matthew	Chrysolite
Thomas	Beryl
James the Less	Topaz
Jude	Chrysoprase
Simon	Hyacinth
Judas	Amethyst

JASPER (left) IS AN AMORPHOUS OPAQUE QUARTZ THAT CAN BE RED, BROWN, GREEN, OR YELLOW. PETRIFIED WOOD IS A VARIETY OF JASPER. MALACHITE (above) HAS THE POWER TO WARD OFF ENCHANTMENTS BECAUSE ITS BRILLIANT GREEN IS THE COLOR OF LIFE, REBIRTH, AND RENEWAL.

© John Pearson/FPG International

emerald for Muriel, sapphire for Herchel, diamond for Humatiel, jacinth for Zuriel, agate for Barbiel, amethyst for Adnachiel, beryl for Humiel, onyx for Gabriel, and jasper for Barchiel. In addition, the ancient Jews held that gemstones were related mystically to the twelve months of the year, the twelve parts of the human body, the twelve hierarchies of the devils, and so on.

In the early Christian era, Saint Jerome noted the coincidental relationship between gemstones and the twelve months of the year and the twelve signs of the Zodiac. He called them the Twelve Apostolic Stones of Christendom.

For some time after Jerome, however, there was no direct relationship established between specific gemstones and birth months. Rather, each person chose a crystal that suited his or her needs. Many people chose certain crystals because of their healing properties—amethyst to ward off intoxication, agate to become agreeable and persuasive, bloodstone as a guard against deception, or malachite as a protection against evil enchantments.

© Rick Cowley

CONTEMPORARY
JEWELRY MAKERS
PROCESS STONES AS
LITTLE AS POSSIBLE.
AT ONE TIME THESE
TOURMALINES
WOULD HAVE BEEN
CUT AND POLISHED
INTO ONE OF THE
TRADITIONAL
FACETED CUTS.
TODAY THEY MIGHT
BE REMOVED FROM
THEIR MASSY SUB-
STRATE AND SET
INTACT INTO SILVER
OR PEWTER RINGS
OR NECK PIECES.

The practice of relating a specific crystal to one's birth month came relatively recently, and probably evolved as an amalgam of all the early correspondences between gems and the number twelve. Today many people believe that birthstones link the cosmic forces of the sky with the crystal energies of the earth, thus maximizing the power of both. They believe astrological forces interlink with crystal energy because the movements of the planets induce particular resonances that crystals absorb and store. Crystals corresponding to a person's zodiac sign are thus held to be a way of attuning an individual body to the flow of energy emanating from the planets.

In this view, birthstones are considered the body's primary receivers of planetary energy. The crystals associated with each zodiacal sign can isolate and direct stellar influences. They also allow other influences to pass through them, amplifying or eliminating those powers according to how their patterns interact with the crystal structure. Hence, following these beliefs, exposure to birthstone crystals can enhance an individual's health.

Over time few changes have been made to the symbology of the original twelve gems the book of Revelations assigns as the foundation stones associated with the twelve apostles. Whether these stones are assigned to the apostles or the signs of the zodiac or the months of the year, the same traditional stones exist in many countries. In the fifteenth century, for example, Italians, Arabs, Jews, and Russians all believed the garnet to be the gem crystal of January.

BIRTHSTONES		**ZODIACAL STONES**	
Month	**Stone***	**Zodiacal Sign**	**Stone***
January	Garnet	Aries	Diamond
February	Amethyst	Taurus	Emerald
March	Aquamarine	Gemini	Pearl
April	Diamond	Cancer	Moonstone
May	Emerald	Leo	Onyx
June	Pearl	Virgo	Sapphire
July	Turquoise	Libra	Tourmaline
August	Sardonyx	Scorpio	Topaz
September	Peridot	Sagittarius	Lapis Lazuli
October	Tourmaline	Capricorn	Ruby
November	Topaz	Aquarius	Aquamarine
December	Ruby	Pisces	Amethyst

*Different lists have evolved over the years; this one is considered the standard list.

Wearing birthstones did not come into common practice until the eighteenth century in Eastern Europe. Originally worn as talismans, birthstones protected the wearer from particular diseases or helped to realize his or her wishes.

Some crystals associated with the seasons are based on obvious associations; for example, emerald for the green months of spring. Emerald also is associated with the planet Venus, which in turn rules Taurus, a spring sign. Moonstone is associated with Cancer because Cancer is a moon-ruled sign; the physical appearance of moonstone is characterized by shimmery light-refracting qualities like those of moonlight or the haziness of a summer afternoon.

As the use of birthstones increased in popularity, affluent people wore a month's birthstone throughout the month, working through all twelve stones in a year and thereby bestowing the benefits of all twelve stones on themselves. Other people would simply wear their own birthstone all year long.

THE LARGE STONE IN EACH OF THESE EARRINGS (right) IS WATERMELON TOURMALINE, A LIBRA STONE. THE SMALLER STONE IS MOONSTONE, WHICH IS GOVERNED BY CANCER. LAPIS LAZULI (opposite page) IS A SAGITTARIUS STONE. IT IS OFTEN USED TO ACCENT OTHER STONES SUCH AS THIS BRILLIANT BLUE-BLACK HEMATITE.

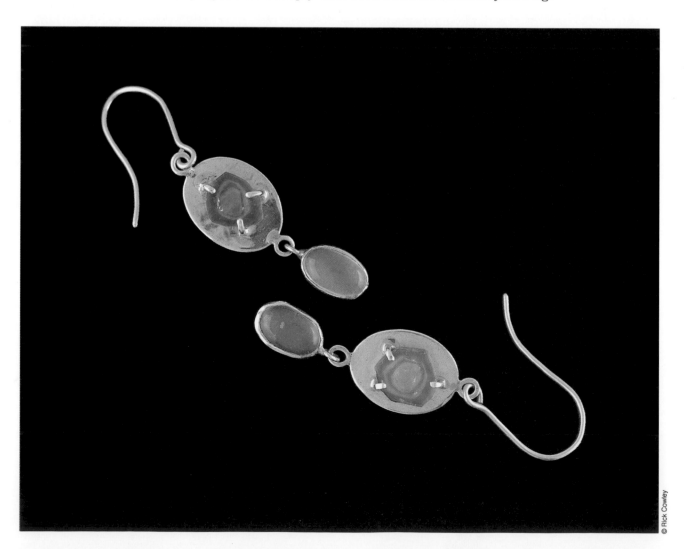

© Rick Cowley

© Rick Cowley

The Lore and Legend of Crystal Balls

To many people the image of the crystal ball calls up fantasies of a comic-strip caricature much more attuned to the finances of her clients than the complexities of the future. The very words *crystal ball* evoke an image of everything that is bogus and sham about the spiritual world.

Yet crystal balls have not always suffered such a bad reputation. They have been found in tombs and funerary urns all over the world. Throughout history people have interpreted the future through reflections. Perhaps the first scryer (gazer) was someone whose attention was captured briefly by the distorted images of the world that appeared in a pool of still water. The first recorded attempts to see into invisible worlds were written after people gazed into a water pot and tried to communicate the meaning of the images there. Scryers came to use whatever they found around them—polished metal, lead droplets, quicksilver (mercury), mirrors, pools of ink, the surfaces of calm ponds.

Crystal balls would seem about the last place to look if you wanted to know how crystals unite the physical with the metaphysical. In nature's hand, crystals emerge in angular, complex, and colorful shapes. In human hands crystal balls take shape as simple and colorless spheres.

THE ANGULAR CLUTTER OF NATURAL CRYSTAL AGGLOMERATIONS HINTS AT THE LIMIT-LESS COMPLEXITY WITHIN ORDERLY STRUCTURES THAT TYPIFIES NATURE. THE DISTINCTIVE COLOR OF THIS SMOKY QUARTZ IS TINGED BY IRON OXIDE.

© Bill Kaunitz

© Bill Kaunitz

THIS CRYSTAL BALL
IS A CLEAR QUARTZ
SPHERE INSIDE
A MIRRORED BOX.
THE TOUCHES OF
BLUE AND GREEN
ARE CAUSED
BY PRISMATIC
REFRACTIONS
INSIDE THE SPHERE.

How a Crystal Ball Is Made

All over the world workers have crafted crystal balls using the same process. The original crystal mass is chipped with a small stone or metal hammer into the shape of a rough sphere. The crystal is then placed inside a metal cylinder along with fragments of emery and garnet to grind it into a precise but unpolished sphere. The cylinder is turned constantly for several days while water periodically washes through it to lubricate the crystal as it smoothes. Finally, it is polished with ground hematite embedded in a soft cloth.

With modern technology, crystal balls are now produced in Germany, France, and the United States. Workers hold the crystal against a rotating grindstone while continually bathing it in water. This turned out to be unhealthy, as many of the men who ground them died of lung ailments.

THE CRYSTAL
ACCORDING TO
HUMANS.

Crystal balls were known in the Middle Ages. Their importance can be gauged by the laborious way in which they were made. Valuable possessions as well as important magical tools, they were passed down from masters to apprentices through many generations.

A crystal ball works by reflecting points of light from its polished surface. Inside the ball the light undergoes distortions that transfix the eye of the gazer until the optic nerve gradually tires. In this way the eye is fooled into thinking that images appear on the surface of the crystal ball. In fact, the images are created when light is distorted on the inside of the crystal ball, and, in effect, plays tricks on the eye of the observer.

The advantage of using a crystal ball rather than an uncut stone is that a sphere optically multiplies reflections and light points so that a person's eye wanders from point to point, suggesting forms and motions in the combinations of numerous reflections.

In a crystal ball a point of light visible to one eye will not be seen by the other, thus disorienting one's sense of binocular vision so that the two images seem to coalesce and move. A good scryer should possess a gifted imagination and be able to visualize pictures similar to those one sees with eyes closed just before sleep. Shifting points of light and repeated reflections of surrounding objects offer a great deal of raw material out of which one can imagine the lifelike visions said to be seen in the crystal. The rest depends on the psychic ability of the gazer.

As the art of gazing developed, crystal balls became the scryer's medium. They consecrated their crystal balls in elaborate rituals. These involved incantations, burying objects in graves, and making the spheres only when the planetary positions were properly aligned. Often young children—presumably innocent of worldly ambitions—were used to read the crystal. Wealthy people and aristocrats kept scryers in their homes just as they did physicians. Queen Elizabeth I consulted a crystal-ball gazer named Dr. Dee many times in search of solutions to political problems.

Most early records of crystal gazing show that the expectations, hopes, or fears of the gazer produced the images revealed in the stone. In many cases the prophetic visions came true because the person who consulted the stone acted on them. Persuaded that what he or she had seen must necessarily come to pass, the gazer proceeded to make the vision come true.

In nineteenth-century England all those who attempted to reveal the hidden secrets of the future were legally designated as rogues. Offenders, on being duly convicted before a justice of the peace, could be sent

© Bill Kaunitz/Courtesy of John Gibbon

© Bill Kaunitz/Courtesy of Pappy & Rosa Mae Gossage

(Left) THE CRYSTAL ACCORDING TO NATURE.

to jail for three months. This ordinance was designed to keep undesirables from using divination to deceive subjects whose proper authority should be the Crown.

The diviners of the Yucatan placed great reliance on "clear stones," probably quartz. To render them suitable for divination purposes the crystals first had to be sanctified according to certain rites. Plant gums were burned before the crystals as magical formulas passed on from one generation of priests to another were recited. When properly cleansed, the diviner claimed to be able to discern the whereabouts of lost objects as well as the activities of people far away.

How To Use a Crystal Ball

STARING AT THIS CRYSTAL BALL NONSTOP FOR A HALF HOUR WILL CAUSE THE EYE TO SEE IMAGES DANCING INSIDE IT.

Most manuals that give instructions on crystal gazing suggest placing the crystal on a table with a black velvet backdrop to protect it from reflections from surrounding objects. Seven lighted candles should be arranged in front of the backdrop, behind the crystal.

Seat yourself comfortably before the crystal, empty your mind of all thoughts, and lay both hands on the ball. Gaze at the crystal continuously for a half hour or more. The light from the candles will produce a multitude of light points in the crystal.

The neophyte gazer should limit the duration of the first experiments to five minutes or so. Prolonged gazing can cause temporary loss of sight. Watery eyes during this time or after the gazing means you have been gazing too long.

When you gaze at the crystal ball successfully, the optic nerve becomes paralyzed to external stimuli and perceives stimuli from the brain. The crystal will seem to disappear and a mist will rise before the eyes, upon which images begin to flicker. The scryer interprets these images.

To maintain psychic contact with the ball when the session is over, put the ball beneath your pillow when you lie down to rest.

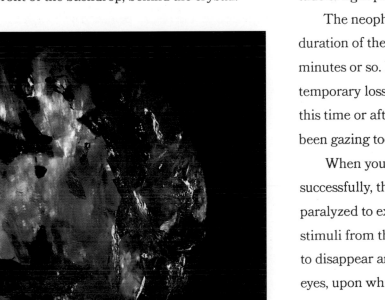

© Bill Kauritz/Courtesy of Enchanted Crystal Store, S.F., CA

Crystal Cosmology

OF THE NINETY-
TWO NATURALLY
OCCURRING
ELEMENTS IN THE
EARTH'S CRUST,
ONLY TWO DOZEN
COMBINE WITH EACH
OTHER IN SUCH A
WAY AS TO PRODUCE
A GEMSTONE, A
ROUGH STONE THAT
CAN BE CUT AND
POLISHED INTO A
GEM AND MOUNTED
AS A JEWEL IN A
RING OR OTHER
SETTING.

Mythmaking has a long history. It seems no natural wonder or product of human thought is free from the human desire to find immortality. As we have seen, the potpourri of anthropology, cultural history, scientific experiment, and New Age speculation that makes up today's crystal lore is no exception.

The Atlantis Legend

One of the most fascinating crystal myths commonly heard today says that the earth's crystals are remnants of a giant crystal that empowered the ancient city of Atlantis. According to the legend, Atlantis vanished eons ago after it destroyed itself by misusing its crystal in an attempt to overpower other nations.

The story originated with Plato. He briefly described Atlantis in his *Timaeus* as a large island in the Atlantic ocean populated with cities named Qest, Phrenegal, Urpurt, and Bisg. As Plato tells it, Atlantis's armies subdued some Mediterranean and African lands, but they were defeated by Athens. Later, great earthquakes and floods shook Atlantis. During a single day and night of rain, Atlantis sank into the sea.

As with many myths, the origins of this story have a plausible basis. Lacking navigational charts, Phoenecian and Greek sailors must have seen many headlands in the mists of the western Mediterranean that they took to be separate islands. Plato probably wrote that Athens defeated Atlantean armies to bolster the spirit of the Attic army and intimidate its enemies. Floods, volcanic eruptions, and earthquakes are common in the Mediterranean; probably few ancient Greeks doubted that whole islands could sink.

Over the years, the mythical city of Atlantis occasionally appeared on sailors' charts and in histories of the ancient world, but lay largely dormant until recently. Today, however, the Atlantis story is a very different tale.

Now the story goes that Atlanteans developed a very sophisticated technological civilization that used crystals to harness the sun's rays to provide free energy to all who lived there. Great crystal grids captured and used the earth's energy field. Controlled thought directed the chemical changes of matter, making it

© Bill Kaunitz

© Bill Kaunitz/Courtesy of Enchanted Crystal Store, S.F., CA

possible to grow huge crystals in very exact shapes. Sound and light were mapped in mental as well as physical frequencies. Crystals powered air, sea, and underwater craft. They also harnessed the powerful reaction between matter and antimatter and thus gave birth to space flight.

THIS THEATRICAL IMAGE (below) IS A SILLY REPRESENTA- TION OF CRYSTAL BALL GAZING— ABOUT AS CLOSE TO GENUINE SCRYING AS RHINESTONES ARE TO DIAMONDS.

In addition, when Atlanteans learned to link crystal power to the mind, humans could travel interdimensionally and through time. Crystals taught the art of perfect concentration, so a workman could visualize a beam of energy miles away to a quarry, lift a stone free of the earth with the beam, transport the stone to a construction site, and fit it without mortar so perfectly that a sheet of paper could not be slipped between the stones. Crystal lighthouses near the sea communicated with dolphins, and operators onshore herded schools of fish into nets waiting offshore. Priests used crystals to experiment with new forms of life, half human and half creature, whence came mermaids, tritons, minotaurs, and centaurs.

© PHOTOWORLD/FPG International

According to today's version of the story, the Atlanteans had one fatal flaw—they never conquered greed. They wanted the wealth of other nations and conquered them using the powers of their gigantic central crystal. But, having vanquished all the lands nearby, they found they could not conquer China, which was on the opposite side of the earth. So they directed their all-powerful crystal to focus its energy straight through the earth to destroy China. The massive energy imbalance that resulted caused enormous earthquakes. In the end, Atlantis destroyed itself with its own power. Bits of the ruptured crystal broke away and floated to the shores of continents far away, where they provide us with the crystals we all use today.

The Meaning of Atlantis

The roots of this modern Atlantis legend go back to the last half of the nineteenth century. Many people were interested in popularized pseudo-scientific entertainments like clairvoyance, crystal-ball reading, séances, and so on. Some purveyors of these entertainments embellished their stories with elaborate revisions of ancient legends.

THE CRYSTAL AND ROCK IN THIS PHOTOGRAPH HAVE NEARLY THE SAME CHEMICAL MAKEUP. THE CRYSTAL HAS BEEN FUSED BY THE ENORMOUS HEAT AND PRESSURE OF THE EARTH'S INTERIOR. THE ROCK IS AN AGGLOMERATION OF PARTICLES THAT HAVE BEEN COMPRESSED INTO STONE BUT NEVER MELTED TO THE POINT OF FUSION.

Then, in the 1940s and 1950s, popular magazines published many articles about the marvels of the scientific world of the future. The scientists in the centuries following the year 2000 would develop time travel, free energy from atomic sources, invisible beams that could transport heavy weights, and many other Atlantislike powers.

By the late 1960s and the 1970s, when New Age ideas began to develop, there was also a general recognition that the possession of great power—for example, atomic fission—could also lead to the destruction of civilization.

The Atlantis story illustrates that legends based on facts and experience often incorporate popular hopes and fears founded on belief rather than facts. It seems the urge to create legends is as strong today as it was in the time of ancient Greece.

What does the blend of crystal history, myth, and speculation have to say about the differences between scientific and New Age thinking?

We can easily accept the fact that crystals have played an important part in the development of modern society. We can accept the possibility that crystals have healing powers because of the persistence of the belief among so many people over so many centuries. But today's Atlantis legend stretches credulity.

New Age thinking has not established a method to separate a plausible idea from wishful thinking. Scientists need to address more experiments to metaphysical phenomena. Both scientists and New Age thinkers could draw on each other's experience and enrich each other's knowledge.

Crystals and the Unity of Experience

Physics attempts to explain the universe on the largest possible scale—from the atomic particle to the immensity of the universe. How do events at the beginning of time determine what will happen at the end of it? How did the laws of nature such as electromagnetism and gravity begin? Physics confines itself to these questions of existence.

Metaphysics studies the role of the spiritual in the universe. It tries to explain our collected body of human knowledge on the largest possible scale—mystical experiences, faith, intuition, religion, daily experience, ethics, the origins of human beliefs, the nature of a supreme being. Metaphysics deals with questions of being.

ALL CRYSTALS CONTAINING URANIUM OXIDE HAVE A YELLOW TINGE. SOME, LIKE THIS AUTUNITE CRYSTAL, ARE BRILLIANT. AUTU-NITE CRYSTALS ARE TOO FRAGILE TO BE MADE INTO JEWELRY, BUT MAKE EXCELLENT DECORATIVE OBJECTS FOR THE HOME OR OFFICE.

© Breck P. Kent

History records our exploring, sampling, codifying, and speculating as we seek understanding. But it is also a description of our attempts to put beauty into sometimes drab recitations of the world's facts. Sometimes, as in the case of Atlantis, we seem to want to hide an uncomfortable truth beneath speculative fantasy; Atlantis's misuse of its giant crystal obviously resembles our efforts with the atom.

Other times proven facts so stretch credibility we are not sure what we can believe any more. Who would have said a few short years ago that cosmologists would discover that the galaxies in the universe are clustered in agglomerations that look like the atoms in an immense crystal?

Yet this is the case. One of the most important jobs of scientists is mapmaking. When astronomers discovered, in 1929, that galaxies are faraway objects, they immediately began to map them. As telescopes and instruments improved, the universe grew larger and more complex. Within the last few years cosmologists have succeeded in mapping large portions of the universe in detail. The resulting strings of galaxies and the voids between them resemble the atomic lattices of crystals.

Crystals have always been objects of both scientific and metaphysical curiosity. Their use by humans has progressed through the stages of life necessity, shamanistic healer, tribal talisman, decorative jewel, and practical tool. They have played a vital role in our material progress. Pottery, fire, pigment, lasers, computer chips—these and many other things came to us by way of crystals.

In short, the seemingly innocuous but pretty crystal has enormous power and significance. It would be tempting to say that crystals were placed here by the gods, but in fact, we know very little about crystal energy, the stones' most godlike attribute.

The New Age idea that spiritual energy is the uniting force of the universe merits more than casual attention. We have grown accustomed to the scientific theory that four fundamental forces (gravity, electromagnetism, the strong force that binds molecules, and the weak force that binds subatomic particles) give the universe its physical structure. Energy fields transmit these forces over distances. The universe is filled with these energy fields. The earth has an energy field, living things have energy fields, and crystals have energy fields. Given these facts, the cosmological discovery that the universe looks like a crystal is not astonishing.

Some ideas presented in this book seem quite logical. We know that crystals are three-dimensional lattices composed of identical atomic structures. Other ideas stretch the boundaries of credibility but are still digestible—for example, the idea that crystal energy fields interact with the transmission of other physical energy. Still other ideas may be hard to swallow. Can crystals really heal spiritual disease by virtue of their ability to channel and harmonize the body's energy system with the universe's energy system?

For whatever reason, crystals seem to have been given a vital role in our understanding of why we are here. In the Introduction of this book crystals are likened to the stained-glass windows in a great cathedral. The scientist observes the patterns of light on the ground and seeks to know the nature of this light based on its colors and patterns and the nature of the ground on which it falls. The metaphysician seeks the meaning of the brilliant images depicted high up in the clerestory; he wants to know what these images represent and the nature of the giant structure holding them in place.

Both scientist and metaphysician produce a valuable knowledge without which a complete understanding of stained glass windows cannot exist. But far more important is the nature of the light before it reaches the window. If it is able to produce all these colors in the window and on the ground, then what color is it? Where does this light come from? And what does it mean?

The fundamental questions about crystals the scientist and metaphysician cannot answer alone but can address together if they share their knowledge.

For Further Reading

Following are a selection of the many books on crystals available:

Achad, Frater. *Crystal Vision Through Crystal Gazing*, 1923. A classic text for crystal gazers.

Adams, John. *A Crystal Source Book: From Science to Metaphysics*, 1988. This book describes the many scientific and metaphysical theories about why crystals appeal to so many people.

Bancroft, Peter. *The World's Finest Minerals and Crystals*, 1973. An exotic picture book for those who appreciate crystals simply for their beauty.

Chesterman, Charles and Kurt Lowe. *The Audubon Field Guide to North American Rocks and Minerals*, 1988. This handy pocket guide tells where to look for crystals, how to unearth them carefully, and how to identify them. Excellent drawings make identification easy.

Court, Arthur. *Minerals: Nature's Fabulous Jewels*, 1987. One of the most beautiful books about the science of crystals.

English, George L. *Getting Acquainted with Minerals*, 1934. If you can find this dowdy, somewhat pedantically written guide, hold on to it as a family heirloom. The "rockhound" bible.

Glazer, A.M. *The Structure of Crystals*, 1987. A concise well-written book. Good for studying the intricate atomic geometry of crystals.

Isaacs, Thelma. *Gemstones, Crystals, and Healing*, 1982. Ms. Isaacs adapts centuries old lore to the New Age philosophy of bodily healing through spiritual healing. An excellent read.

Kunz, George F. *Gems and Precious Stones of North America*, 1892 (Dover reprint, 1968). Another very good field guide of the *Audubon* variety.

Loomis, Frederick. *Field Book of Common Rocks and Minerals*, 1948. Goes beyond crystals to the rocks in which they are found.

Prince, Thessalonia. *Six Lessons in Crystal Gazing*, 1986. A detailed exploration of the more subtle aspects of crystal gazing.

Prinz, Martin, George Harlow, and Joseph Peters. *Simon & Schuster's Guide to Rocks and Minerals*, revised 1978. Another fine book for the hiker/crystal hobbyist. Good color drawings and concise text.

Robinson, Marlene. *Crystals: What They Are and How to Grow Them*, 1988. A straightforward discussion of how to make crystals.

Sorrell, Charles, and George Sandstrom. *Golden's Field Guide to Identifying Rocks and Minerals*, 1973. Not as elaborate as the Audubon, Dover, or Simon & Schuster guides, but inexpensive and excellent for the occasional hobbyist.

Wind, Wabun, and Anderson Reed. *Light Seeds: A Compendium of Ancient and Modern Crystal Knowledge*, 1988. An extended excursion into the byways and freeways of crystal lore.

Crystal Collections and Related Magazines

For research or just for sheer viewing pleasure, there are many outstanding crystal collections across the United States located in university geology departments.

To find the collections in your area, consult the U.S. Geological Survey office, in Washington, D.C. There are also thousands of hobbyists with superb collections. Many of them advertise in the periodicals listed below:

Body, Mind, and Spirit
P.O. Box 701
Providence, RI 02901

Earth Science
4220 King Street
Alexandria, Va 22301-1507

Jewelry Making: Gems and Minerals
P.O. Box 226
Cortaro, AZ 85652-0226

Lapidary Journal
P.O. Box 80937
San Diego, CA 92138

Mineralogical Record
4630 Paseo Tabutama
Tucson, AZ 85740

Music of the Spheres
P.O. Box 12751
Taos, NM 87571

New Age Journal
342 Western Avenue
Brighton, MA 02135

Rocks and Minerals
4000 Albermarle Street N.W.
Washington, D.C. 20016

Whole Earth Review
27 Gate Five Road
Sausalito, CA 94965

Whole Life
P.O. Box 2058
New York, NY 10159

Index

Page numbers in italics
refer to captions
and illustrations.